ool ... the College or University then existing in the City of Durham a University ...
Cathedral Church and for ever thereafter to continue and be a University by ...
same should consist of a Warden or Principal a Professor of Divinity and ...
Mathematics and two Proctors and of such Readers and Teachers the same ...
respectively and of such Graduates in the several Faculties and of such ...
versity and do in all other respects confirm the said Act of Chapter of ...
ous and Proceedings which had been made and had pursuant thereto ...
blishment of the said University and amongst others the following ...
That the first or present Convocation shall consist of the said Charles Thorp ...
three Faculties or of Master of Arts in any of the Universities of Oxford Cambridge ...
ature shall consist besides the original members of all persons regularly admitted ...
Arts in the University of Durham and conforming to the Regulations ...
admission of Members of the said University that is to say No one shall be ...
has not been placed on the Register of the University by the authority of the Warden ...
John Banks by Divine Permission Bishop of St David's Dean and the Chapter of ...
nors of the said University of Durham and the said Charles Thorp the Warden of ...
dition to the endowment provided by the lastly mentioned Act of Parliament relating ...
you made thereto And also that many students have resorted to the said University and ...
Literature And also that the said Charles Thorp is the present Warden of the said ...
that the said Temple Chevallier is the present Professor of Mathematics That the ...
n Thorp and divers other Doctors and Masters in the several Faculties to the number of ...
bridge Robert Warwick Iuness John Cundill and others to the number of seventy one ...
sity during the Academical Terms and actively engaged in their respective duties And ...
lam and the wants of the surrounding Districts are assured that with the blessing of ...
Religious Principles but that they are advised that the said University would be ...
Members were incorporated by Our Royal Charter And have humbly prayed us ...
ers of the said University of Durham and all persons who shall hereafter be duly ...
may become and be for ever hereafter one Body Politic and Corporate **Now know** ...
learning and trusting that the said University of Durham so established under our ...
an eminent source of good to our loving subjects especially in the northern parts of our ...
declared and appointed And by these presents for us our heirs and successors Do ...
who shall hereafter be duly admitted Members of the said University in pursuance ...
ter made and established by the said Dean and Chapter under their Common ...
Members thereof shall be and remain for ever hereafter One Body Politic and ...
ars of the University of Durham" And by that name shall ...
a new such Seal from time to time at their will and pleasure And by that ...
ment made and passed in the third year of our Reign and by that name shall ...
the University therein contemplated and authorized or are distinct to a University ...
e Patent **Witness** ourself at Our Palace at Westminster the first day of June in ...

r Seal

Edmunds

The Durham difference

The Durham difference

THE STORY OF DURHAM UNIVERSITY

NIGEL WATSON

JAMES
X
JAMES

© The University of Durham,
trading as Durham University 2007
First published 2007
ISBN 978 1 903942 78 9

James & James (Publishers) Ltd
2-5 Benjamin Street
London EC1M 5QL

Editor: Susan Millership
Designer: Robin Farrow
New photography: Malcolm Crowthers

Printed and bound by
Butler & Tanner,
Frome, Somerset

Publisher's acknowledgements

James & James would like to thank Dr Michael Stansfield
for his tremendous support, expert advice and good
humour during the production of *The Durham difference*
as well as Richard Brickstock, Curator of the Castle,
Michele Allan from the Design and Imaging Unit and Ann
Boyd at *The Northern Echo*. The advice and support of
Liesl Elder, and her team in the University's Development
and Communications office, have been crucial throughout.

Contents

Acknowledgements

This book claims to be no more than a sweeping summary of the birth, infancy and maturity of one of the country's leading universities. A mountain of documentary material, as well as the untapped reminiscences of staff and students, past and present, awaits the author of the definitive history of Durham University.

This story relies heavily on the work and contributions of other people. The first part of the story, from foundation until the new constitution of 1937, owes much to previous histories by J T Fowler and C E Whiting, to the numerous college histories in existence and to more recent contributions to the early history of the University. I am also in the debt of Alan Heesom and David Watkinson, who freely gave me their advice and opinions, drawn from their own research.

The greater part of the book tells the story of the real growth of the University from 1937 onwards. The minutes of Council and Senate, with the annual reports made by the Warden, were prime sources, as was the complete run of the University newspaper, Palatinate, which proved particularly useful for a student view of the University's development. These were supplemented by a variety of other material. In particular, I had the advantage of discussing the more recent past with the current Vice-Chancellor and his two immediate predecessors, as well as a number of senior University staff.

Throughout this project I had the unfailing and invaluable assistance and advice of Dr Michael Stansfield, the University archivist, Dr Richard Higgins, his colleague, and other staff of the University Library's Archives and Special Collections. I am also grateful for the hospitality I enjoyed from my own college, Castle. The final version of the text also owes much to the suggestions and guidance of Susan Millership and Alison Austen.

It has been a privilege to return to Durham and discover so much about it that I never knew. It has been an awesome undertaking, knowing that the project would fall under the scrutiny of Alan Heesom, whose memorable lectures formed part of my own degree in history at Durham. Any shortcomings, of course, remain my responsibility, but I hope this limited survey at least suggests that I learned some of the lessons delivered by Alan and his colleagues more years ago now than I care to recall.

Nigel Watson, May 2007

Chancellor's Foreword

It is my private conviction that you can tell that you are in a good university town from the moment of arrival, in much the way you can often sense the presence of the sea before you actually see it. There's just something in the air – a passing waft of cerebral pheromones perhaps.

And nowhere that I know of is that happy air of productive, brainy toil more winningly offset by architectural glory than in Durham. What other universities, after all, can claim a castle and cathedral at their very heart or boast that they inhabit a World Heritage site? (Well, none, to be ungraciously frank.) Thanks to its heaps of stony splendour, Durham was always certain to be a place of deep appeal, but how splendid that so much of its glorious space is devoted to tracking down facts and honing fine minds. What better way to fill so much ancient fabric than with the buzz of intellectual pursuits?

I must confess that I was excited and intrigued, as I am sure you are, to see what this book contains.

Bill Bryson

Wolfson Research Institute

Vice-Chancellor's Foreword

This book provides a showcase for one of the world's historic Universities. Durham University, the third oldest in England, was a place of scholarship and influence for a millennium before the University was formally established. It is the only University based in a world heritage site. As a result of its history and environment, Durham University has a unique and distinctive sense of place and community.

Durham University has given much, and has much more to offer, to the development of our society, economy and communities. We have an enviable reputation as a research-led university and a unique collegiate system which delivers a distinctive educational experience. The University is now a diverse community of some of the world's leading scholars and thinkers, and more than 15,000 of the world's most talented students. Durham University alumni play leadership roles in all walks of life, both high-profile and low-key, throughout the world.

Today, Durham's student body is socially diverse with staff and students from over 120 countries around the globe. This diverse community lives and works together in a unique collegiate environment which offers freedom, inclusivity, participation, the opportunity to develop personal identity and leadership, and a sense of belonging – a true symbol of the 'Durham difference'

Our scholarship and research is renowned across traditional academic disciplines in science, arts and humanities, and the social sciences. Our research is helping to shape the world we share from the understanding of galaxies, to issues of public health, education, social geography and medical science – from literature to psychology, music to migration. But it is people that remain at the heart of our community and their contribution is noted throughout this book.

As Durham's 23rd Vice-Chancellor and Warden, I am proud and honoured by the responsibility of leading the University into its second 175 years but, more than that, as a former student, to have returned 'home' to such a wonderful place and institution.

Professor Chris Higgins

Grey towers of Durham; begirt by winding Wear,
Well yet I love thy mixed and massive pile,
Half church of God, half castle, 'gainst the Scot
and long to roam these venerable aisles,
with records stored of deeds long since forgot.

Sir Walter Scott, 1816.

Cuthbert to Van Mildert: before 1832

DURHAM IS A MAGICAL PLACE. To catch a glimpse from the train of the majestic Norman cathedral and the picturesque castle, observed the writer J B Priestley, is to see one of the finest views in England. It is a view familiar to countless generations of students, for whom Durham means the university where they were privileged to spend three years of their lives.

An ancient city, steeped in history, Durham's links with education stretch back almost a thousand years. Durham University has not been around quite so long, although its foundation in 1832 makes it England's third oldest university. Its story is one of triumph over adversity, seizing opportunities, building on success and having faith in the power of a university to inspire the mind, sustain ideals and deliver the common good. Born out of political expediency as much as high-minded principle, reluctant to break out of its ecclesiastical insulation and embrace the industrial world around it, the University of Durham has become one of the strongest universities in the country. Sustained by a collegiate system quite unlike any other, and by a handful of dedicated dons, Durham entered the twentieth century linked to its offspring in Newcastle. The final separation of the two institutions in 1963 acted as a catalyst for Durham's further growth. Negotiating the obstacles thrown in its path by the unpredictable nature of government policy, Durham emerged bruised but strengthened in the 1990s. The elements of today's University were already there – a commitment to high standards of research, an enthusiasm to reach out beyond the boundaries of academia into the wider world and a willingness to open the doors of the University to those who might never even have dreamt of entering. As Durham moves into the twenty-first century, all those strands have been woven tightly together to produce a university of international standing.

Durham's educational links have followed a long monastic tradition. In 995 Durham became a place of pilgrimage when the relics of St Cuthbert, having evaded the plundering Vikings for several centuries, were finally laid to rest. Only a few years later, the bones of the Venerable Bede, the father of English history, were also brought to Durham. Generations of scholars at the University have found tranquillity and inspiration from contemplation of the saint's tomb in the Galilee Chapel of Durham's magnificent cathedral. A World Heritage site, the cathedral has dominated the city since building first began in 1093, not just physically, but also temporally and spiritually, through the power and influence of the so-called Prince Bishops. These powerful clerics, properly styled Counts Palatine, ruled on behalf of the monarch within their diocese until Tudor times, and did not give up all their secular influence until the 1830s. It was the last of the prince bishops, William Van Mildert, who created the University of Durham.

The clerics of the diocese also influenced the early development of the University of Oxford, helping to found University College and Balliol College in the thirteenth century. Durham Hall, later Durham College, was founded at much the same time, but lasted only until the dissolution of the monasteries, when the site and the buildings became the home of another new college, Trinity. The dissolution in Durham brought the replacement of the Prior by the Dean and Chapter, but this lasted barely a century before their temporary abolition during the time of Oliver Cromwell. Cromwell's claim to be an educational benefactor in the city is still championed by some in Durham and on at least two occasions his name has been put forward for new colleges in the University.

In 1650 the departure of the Dean and Chapter prompted a petition to Parliament, by some of the county's most influential men, to use the vacant deanery properties to create a college for the education of their own sons. But Parliament procrastinated and the petitioners appealed directly to Cromwell. He was sympathetic, writing to the Speaker that 'truly it seems to me a matter of great concern-

William Van Mildert, co-founder of the University in 1832 and Durham's last Prince Bishop. He left his residence, Durham Castle, to the University on his death in 1837.

ment and importance, as that which (by the blessing of God) may much conduce to the promotion of learning and piety in these poor, rude and ignorant parts'.[1] The Protector, however, had more pressing matters on his mind and it was only in May 1657 that Letters Patent were issued for the new college. These failed to grant the power to confer degrees, so the college managed to persuade Cromwell's successor, his son Richard, to issue instructions to draw up a charter. This roused the ire of the two established universities. Lawyers were engaged, petitions drawn up and deputations despatched. Another university, it was said, conferring more degrees, would devalue those given by existing universities and produce graduates of inferior quality. Richard Cromwell caved in. With Oxbridge triumphant, the Protectorate in its death throes, and the restoration of the monarchy imminent, the life of the college came to an end early in 1660. The only evidence of this brief episode is the name that has persisted ever since for the buildings in the cathedral close – The College.

The idea of creating an institution of higher learning in Durham was revived nearly two centuries later only because the Church believed it offered a solution to its current difficulties. The irony was that the founder of England's third university, the holder of an ecclesiastical office, a man of extreme conservative views, came from the very classes pressing hardest for reform and suffered from snobbery for much of his life because of his origins. The founder of the University of Durham may have been the last of the prince bishops, but he was also the son of an unsuccessful gin distiller.

William Van Mildert came to Durham as bishop in 1826. Unlike his predecessor, Shute Barrington, the son of a viscount whose preferment came through family connections, Van Mildert's career was a triumph of talent and intellect over modest beginnings and financial embarrassment. He came close to bankruptcy once and his future parents-in-law thought so little of his prospects that for several years they refused to give their consent for him to marry their daughter. But his natural ability and fluent defence of the Church earned him the appointment in 1813 as Regius Professor of Divinity at Oxford, and then, in 1819, his preferment as Bishop of Llandaff. Unlike his predecessors, Van Mildert actually lived in the diocese. In 1820 he gave up Oxford to become Dean of St Paul's, holding the office alongside his bishopric. As Bishop of Durham, he divided his time between the diocese, his London residence and Harrogate, where he often took the waters as his health declined.

1 Quoted in Whiting, C E, *The University of Durham 1832–1932*, London, 1932, p. 18.

Top, Early exams in Cosin's Library 1842. *Middle,* Illustrations of University College by Cuthbert Bede, 1840s; *left,* a student study, *right,* preparing for dinner, *Bottom,* Students of University College on the steps of the Castle Great Hall entrance, c.1898.

Facing page, The Tunstal Gallery in University College today, *above*, painted by Cuthbert Bede in the 1840s.

Van Mildert was keenly interested in education, doing his utmost in Oxford to encourage his students, supporting, as Bishop of Llandaff, the foundation of St David's College, Lampeter, and as Bishop of Durham, King's College London. Although he kept up the style of the prince bishops (it came with the job), as someone who had experienced near-penury, he was determined to apply diocesan funds to better effect. He gave money to numerous good causes, including the support of Church schools in the county, fervently believing that education should be at the core of the Church's mission to the poor. The bishop's interest in education proved instrumental in the birth of the University of Durham.

The pressure for alternatives to the unreformed universities of Oxford and Cambridge had already seen the foundation of University College London. With its non-denominational character, it was a rebuff to Oxbridge's exclusive Anglican club, where degrees were granted only to those subscribing to the Thirty-Nine Articles. In the north, the country's leading Whig politician and advocate of reform, Earl Grey, had given his

A passionate advocate of a northern English university, the 2nd Earl Grey, a leading politician and reformer.

support to the idea of a new university based in either Newcastle or Durham.

It was the idea of using part of the diocese's riches to do this that whetted many radical appetites. Even Van Mildert, the most conservative of bishops, realised that the Church would have to change. In Durham the wealth and corruption of the establishment had been at the heart of the election in 1830 that brought Grey to power. Embarking on parliamentary reform, which many saw as the precursor to ecclesiastical reform, Grey warned the bishops 'to set their house in order and prepare to meet the coming storm'.[2] It was, wrote Charles Thorp, the bishop's principal adviser and later Archdeacon of Durham, 'a feverish and hapless time'.[3]

The idea that the Church should take the lead in founding a northern university first came from Thorp in the summer of 1831.[4] Although he shared Van Mildert's conservative views, he had also been Grey's chaplain for a time and understood the need to bridge the political divide in the Church's interest. For Van Mildert, it was an ideal way of deflecting public and political criticism.

2 Quoted in Heesom, A, 'The Founding of the University of Durham', *Durham Cathedral Lecture*, 1982, p. 21.
3 Rev. Charles Thorp to James Losh, 12 September 1831, *Thorp Correspondence*, 49.
4 See Heesom, A, 'Who Thought of the Idea of the University of Durham', *Durham County Local History Society Bulletin* 29, 1982.

For the same reasons, the idea also had the support of the Dean, Charles Jenkinson. Their combined influence persuaded more doubtful members of the Chapter to back the scheme when it was revealed to all of them on 28 September 1831. Thorp, writing the following month, was confident that 'this establishment is likely to be a leading feature of the north of England, and will probably obtain much celebrity in the way of education at home and abroad'.[5]

Thorp drew up the details while Van Mildert set about winning political support. The new university was backed by the Archbishop of Canterbury, William Howley, and by many of the reformers, the latter less radical than the public thought and happy to see the Church reforming itself. The University of Durham Act became law on 4 July 1832.

It was a smooth piece of politics from the bishop. The Act devoted Church funds to the endowment of the University, but it ensured that only Anglicans could proceed to degrees, a requirement not entirely removed until religious tests in universities were abolished in 1871. Control over the University also remained with the Church through the Dean and Chapter, as the University Statutes of 1834 confirmed, while the bishop retained the role of chief arbiter as Visitor. Thorp, the architect of the scheme, which was modelled on Christ Church, Oxford, became the first Warden of the University. There was a Senate that transacted ordinary academic business and originated other measures, which were either confirmed or rejected by a Convocation made up of all members of the University with degrees above the Bachelor of Arts (BA). One pioneering feature, later universal in British universities outside Oxbridge, was the regular appointment of external examiners to maintain the standard of degrees.

The conservative influence of Oxbridge was inevitably in evidence, since every clergyman in Durham had graduated from one of the two ancient universities. Thorp framed the statutes with help from Canon Samuel Smith, another Oxford graduate, recently arrived in Durham from his previous post as Dean of Christ Church, Oxford. The curriculum, based on the classics with mathematics, owed much to Oxbridge, and the first post-holders were Oxbridge graduates. From the very beginning, Durham, like Oxford and Cambridge, was a residential university, with University College starting life in Cosin's Hall in 1832. But the new university would differ from Oxbridge in one significant way. In 1837 University College (usually known simply as

John Cundill, the first student of the University, 1836.

Temple Chevallier, Professor of Mathematics, masterminded the introduction of engineering and astronomy at Durham.

Castle) moved into Durham Castle but, unlike Oxbridge, not as an independent corporate body for, by an Order in Council, the building was vested in the bishop to hold in trust for use by the University. Similarly, the colleges which followed Castle in Durham have never been independent corporate bodies.

When the first foundation students came to Durham in October 1833, most of them took rooms in Archdeacon's Inn, now Cosin's Hall, on Palace Green. The students were John Cundill (who three years later became the first holder of a first class from Durham), St Clere Raymond, Henry Stoker, John Treacy, Robert Pratt, Morton Eden Wilson, Henry Press Wright, George Marshall, John Francis Erskine, James Skinner, Frederick Brewster Thompson, Henry Humble, Ralph Errington, Thomas Maddison, William Thomas Watson, John Yarker, James Watson Hick, William Bramwell Ferguson and George Hill.[6] Alongside them were eighteen ordinary students and five divinity students.

On 1 June 1837 the University was finally awarded its charter. This was largely thanks to the efforts of Earl Grey, who, in return, received Durham's first honorary degree the following year.

Underfunded from the beginning, the University struggled to attract students. Yet, even though numbers between 1832 and 1862 peaked at only 130 (in the early 1850s), Durham survived.

Attempts were made to offer courses attractive to students intending to pursue a career in the industries on the University's doorstep. In 1838 Durham became the first English university to offer courses in civil and mining engineering. Temple Chevallier, the Professor of Mathematics, was the brains behind this. He was supported by James Johnston, the Reader in Chemistry. Johnston, one of the founders of the British Association for the Advancement of Science in 1831, believed strongly in the value of practical experimentation. As a result, Durham had some of the earliest scientific laboratories in the country. Chevallier was also responsible for the introduction of astronomy in 1839, raising the funds to build the observatory completed in 1842. By 1840 there were more engineering students than theology students, but this success was short-lived. The course, coupled with residential expenses, was too costly. Many students could not afford to complete their third year. Those who did achieve the aca-

5 Quoted in Heesom, 'The Founding of the University of Durham', p. 32.
6 First Calendar, 1833, in *Documents Relating to the Establishment of Durham University and of University College Therein*, Durham, 1902, Appendix 4, p. 31.

Raising the College flag at the Castle is steeped in tradition; the winner of a race from the courtyard to the top of the Keep and back decides who will have the job of 'the College flag' for the year. Being 'the College flag' involves hoisting the flag to mark formal College dinners on Tuesdays and Thursdays and on the Master's birthday.

Rowing at Durham has a long history; this University Boat Club crew dates from 1860.

Council in November 1909. Dean Kitchin became the first Chancellor, the post of Vice-Chancellor was created, the University was divided into two divisions, the Durham Division and the Newcastle Division, and the ownership of all property in Durham was handed over to the new Council of Durham Colleges. The Act's weakness was that it was driven by the need to give Newcastle a say within the University, so it did little to give the University an effective structure for strategic development. Once again, the two separate parts of the University were more powerful than the whole. In Durham, the Council of Durham Colleges covered only three colleges, University, Hatfield and the women's college, later St Mary's. It had no jurisdiction over three-fifths of students, in the teacher training colleges of Bede and St Hild's, and the private Anglican halls of residence, St John's and St Chad's. Yet this uneasy balance between the three parts of the University actually fostered a partnership between lay and academic interests that, for the most part, avoided the conflict which plagued some other civic universities.

Frisbee on Palace Green.

PLEASE KEEP OFF THE GRASS

The River Wear from Prebend's Bridge inscribed with
Sir Walter Scott's words about Durham.

Seeking Solutions: 1910–37

FOR THE NEXT TWENTY-FIVE YEARS the intricate constitution devised by the 1908 Act provided a framework for
steady progress in Newcastle and a cautiously conservative
approach in Durham towards a broader university education. Newcastle created a wide range of new chairs at both
Armstrong College (including history, economics, naval architecture,
electrical engineering and geography) and the College of Medicine.
Durham appointed Professors of English Language and Literature,
Latin, Logic and Psychology, Philosophy and Modern Languages.
Students taking the new three-year BA no longer had to study
Greek; they could choose Latin instead. Many of Durham's new
chairs were filled from within the University, and the Professor of
Astronomy was not replaced when Ralph Sampson was appointed
Astronomer Royal for Scotland in 1910.

The First World War interrupted the development of both divisions of the University. The College of Medicine turned out doctors
for the front, while Armstrong College was requisitioned for use as
a military hospital. The dwindling number of wartime students dis-
persed elsewhere. In Durham, Hatfield Hall, Cosin's Hall and St
John's College were all temporarily commandeered. Students and
staff from Newcastle and Durham, including the officers and men
of the University's Officer Training Corps (OTC), went to war. From
the University as a whole, 2,500 served in the war, of whom 325

Shooting Eight, 1914.

never returned. In Durham, OTC members who had not been called up were allowed to attend lectures in uniform, so long as they wore academic dress after dusk. Leave of absence was granted to all those on national service, scholarship holders were told they would be able to take up their scholarships on their return and students on military service were granted three terms' exemption towards their degrees, provided they completed at least six terms. Societies fell dormant, sporting activities ground to a halt, June Week was abandoned and there was a temporary merger of the Union Societies in Durham and Newcastle. By 1916 there were so few students in Durham that the Council asked its secretary, Professor Robinson, to issue a notice scotching public rumours that it was about to close. Durham was so strapped for cash that it made a vain request for state aid. In Newcastle, Armstrong College was on the verge of bankruptcy.

The University's finances worsened after the war. In the early 1920s Durham Castle began sliding down the hill into the river Wear. Restoration was estimated to cost £30,000 (more than £1 million today), twice the annual income of the colleges and easily exceeding the funds available. It was a bill that almost crippled the University. Relief came only with the eventual launch of a public appeal in the late 1920s. Much of the burden of the restoration was shouldered by Percy Heawood, Vice-Chancellor between 1924 and 1926, who at times fought practically single-handedly to stop the castle falling down. He also became

17 Council of Durham Colleges (CDC) minutes, 10 December 1929.

the driving force behind the Durham Castle Preservation Committee, which campaigned almost incessantly to raise funds. With the original appeal raising £24,000, the Committee added another £75,000 between 1929 and 1934, the equivalent of almost £4.5 million today. It was a truly Herculean effort, but one which had still not come to an end by 1939.

The crisis at the castle did not deter Durham from thinking seriously about its future. The process began during the war and the Council drew up a list of priorities in 1917. New colleges, improvements to existing colleges, more lecturers and more scholarships to attract increasing numbers of students were on the list. But these plans soon became more ambitious. Although the student body remained an elite, less than 1 per cent of the eligible age group, there were more students at university than ever before. Total student numbers in the UK had risen from 14,000 in 1900 to 34,000 in 1920. The University of Durham had 1,100, but nearly 900 of them were in Newcastle. Durham was tiny and needed to grow. The two Anglican halls of residence, St Chad's and St John's, both became constituent colleges of the University in 1923, but this only formalised an existing arrangement. A request for state funding was swiftly despatched from the Council of Durham Colleges to the Board of Education. The Council wanted to create more scholarships, expand the arts, improve provision for the increasing number of student teachers and introduce science teaching. Science was seen as essential after the war if Durham was going to be 'of real service to the life and industries of the County and beyond'.[17]

Scaffolding on the Castle – major restoration works began in the 1920s to stop the medieval Castle slipping into the River Wear.

Percy John Heawood, Professor of Mathematics, Hebrew scholar and Vice-Chancellor, spearheaded the campaign to save the Castle for which he received an OBE. He joined the University in 1887 and retired 52 years later.

Facing page, Appeal poster produced by Durham Castle Preservation Fund. By 1934 the cost of restoration had reached the equivalent of £4.5 million at today's rates.

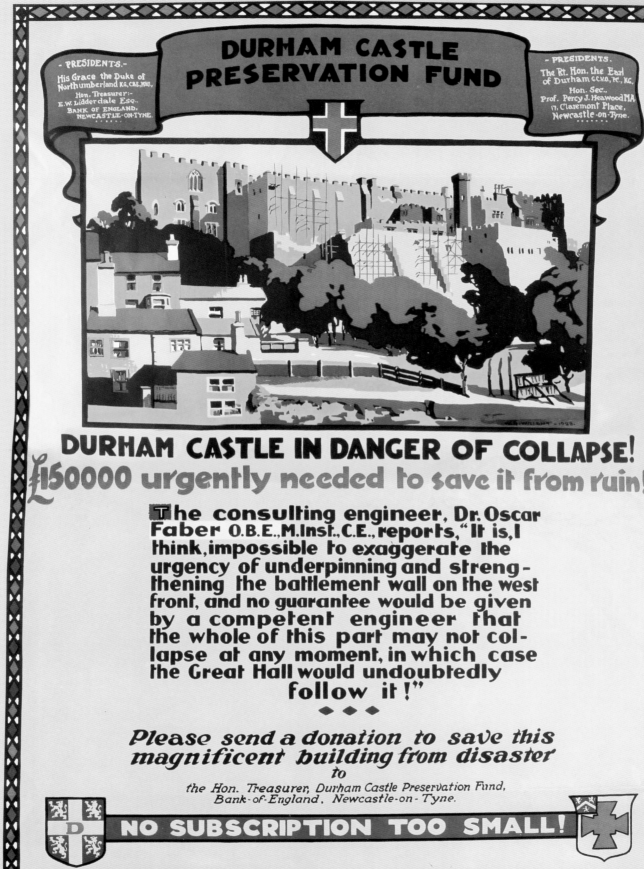

DURHAM CASTLE PRESERVATION FUND

DURHAM CASTLE IN DANGER OF COLLAPSE!

£150000 urgently needed to save it from ruin!

The consulting engineer, Dr. Oscar Faber O.B.E., M.Inst., C.E., reports, "It is, I think, impossible to exaggerate the urgency of underpinning and strengthening the battlement wall on the west front, and no guarantee would be given by a competent engineer that the whole of this part may not collapse at any moment, in which case the Great Hall would undoubtedly follow it!"

◆ ◆ ◆

Please send a donation to save this magnificent building from disaster

to

the Hon. Treasurer, Durham Castle Preservation Fund,
Bank-of-England, Newcastle-on-Tyne.

 NO SUBSCRIPTION TOO SMALL!

A common sight. A cormorant on a favoured spot on the Wear.

'If you have never been to
Durham, go there at once.
Take my car. It's wonderful.'
Bill Bryson

A classic view of Durham – the
River Wear, Framwellgate
Bridge, Castle and Cathedral.

In fact, the University Grants Committee (UGC) told the Council in January 1921 that there would be no money unless Durham was more ambitious. The UGC was also reluctant to give money to a University which was pouring a lot of it into restoring a historical monument, but it was impressed by the willingness of the Council to take up suggestions for economies. University College was losing money, so the Council agreed to the UGC's recommendation that the administration and services of University and Hatfield Colleges should be merged. This encouraged the UGC to increase its annual grant to the Durham colleges and provide a one-off contribution which helped to build new lecture rooms and expand the library in the late 1920s.

Durham's response to the demand from the UGC to be more ambitious focused on two interlinked developments – a school of pure science and an education department. Durham had already licensed Bede College (and another training college, Neville's Cross) as a hall of residence, with the intention that it should become the nucleus of the planned department of education. Bede was later renamed the College of the Venerable Bede in 1935. St Hild's too was important to the University for the same reason, as a source of trainee teachers.

Teacher training was in the throes of reform after the war. University education departments moved away from teaching non-graduates to a four-year teacher training course, comprising a three-year degree plus a one-year postgraduate qualification. In Durham the Council of Durham Colleges was already working towards this, in collaboration with the county council. But the county council was especially concerned to obtain teachers who were science graduates, and was willing to commit a halfpenny rate, amounting annually to £8,500 (£300,000 in today's terms), towards the development of science in Durham. The UGC also gave its support for a science school, and Sir Theodore Morison, the new Principal of Armstrong College, said the college would not oppose such a move so long as Durham did not move into applied science. A joint board, unique among British universities, was formed, with at least half its members from the county council.

The Council of Durham Colleges gave ten acres of land on the south side of the city for the new science buildings. Housing chemistry, physics, botany and geology, with laboratory accommodation for ninety students, the buildings were named after County Durham's Director of Education, Sir Arthur Dawson, and opened by the distinguished scientist, Sir William Bragg, in October 1924. It was a grand occasion – a band played as university dignitaries and other guests processed from the science site via Prebend's Bridge to the Great Hall of Durham Castle for tea. It was also one of the most significant events in the development of the University.

Teacher training was important because it gave Durham the additional students it sorely needed. In 1935 there were still only 475 students (and 1,155 at Newcastle), but this was more than twice the number in 1920. Of these, 149 were students of the training colleges, and 103 were women. Durham's new science department depended on the teacher training programme. In 1927, for instance, almost every science graduate went into teaching. But science also gave Durham the academic ballast it had lacked for so long. The foundation of the world-class science Durham boasts today dates back to the department's beginnings in 1924. The quality of staff in this small department was outstanding. Between the wars the trend in British universities was for interest in academic science to wane. In Durham, the reverse was the case. The striking early success of the department was achieved partly through the willing help of the science departments in Newcastle. Half of all Durham's science students (there were 82 in 1929) were studying for honours, with most of them achieving first or second class degrees. The ten staff appointed to the department were among the first in Durham with a responsibility to carry out research as well as to teach. Over the first five years they published fifty research papers. This early success led to the adoption in 1929 of a two-phase building programme, but the money ran out, so only one phase was completed.

The opening of the science site caused great excitement in Durham. Until 1924 the academic world in Durham had revolved around Palace Green. The science site was a world which staff involved in teaching theology and the arts found almost impossible to understand. The science staff, on the other hand, had no qualms about questioning Durham's status quo. Two of its outstanding figures were Arthur Holmes and Irvine Masson.

Arthur Holmes arrived in Durham as Reader in Geology, aged thirty-four. He was appointed Professor a year later. A visionary geologist, he already had an established reputation and a string of impressive research papers and books to his name. This was in spite of the fact that he was hindered by a serious shortage of equipment. Yet he had been jobless and living in Gateshead in virtual poverty for nine months before Durham revived his academic career. Under these trying circumstances, Holmes employed his genius in pioneering isotope geology and geochronology. Using radioactivity to date rock formations, he made important advances in estimating the age of the earth. He also helped to validate the theory of continental drift, developed largely while he was at Durham, but this was controversial and he failed to win the credit he deserved during his lifetime. His work in Durham was commemorated in 2001, when the new isotope laboratory was named in his honour. Quietly spoken, kindly and unassuming, he was an inspiring teacher who, with his junior colleague, attracted many students to switch to geology from their original choice of subject. The textbook, *Principles of Physical Geology,* on which he began work while at Durham, was published in 1943 and became an international best-seller. This, said one of his most famous students, Sir Kingsley Dunham (himself later Professor of Geology at Durham), was 'a challengingly original exposition', presenting 'a philosophy of the whole earth'. For Dunham, Holmes was 'one of the greatest geologists of the century'.[18] Rarely seen at learned societies or international gatherings, he was elected a Fellow of the Royal Society in 1942.

Archaeology came to Durham in 1931 with the appointment of Eric Birley as lecturer.

The first Professor of Chemistry, and head of the science department, was Irvine Masson. Born in Melbourne, Australia, in 1887, Masson's father and grandfather had both been professors. His father, Sir David Masson, had emigrated to Melbourne on his appointment as Professor of Chemistry and became an outstanding figure in Australian science. Masson, like Wagstaff, had worked during the war on research at the Royal Arsenal. Prior to his arrival in Durham he had been on the staff of the chemistry department at University College London. Many years later, his obituarist in the *Durham University Journal* portrayed him almost as a man with a split personality, personally polite and genial, helpful and fair, yet someone who found Durham challenging, and exacerbated rather than ameliorated the differences between those on the science site and those on Palace Green. Yet he stayed in Durham for fourteen years, which suggests he found it a sufficiently congenial place to work. A strong personality, he was the ideal man to lead an infant department. Within his department he encouraged colleagues to pursue their own research and shared staff with them. He 'acted on the principle that Durham, being new in the field of chemistry, could not afford to give cheap degrees'.[19] He left Durham for the post of Vice-Chancellor of Sheffield University in 1938. In the following year he was elected a Fellow of the Royal Society and was knighted in 1950. He left the science department in Durham so strong on his departure that his post as head of department was abolished.

The progress of science at Durham between the wars outshone any achievements in the arts and humanities. The only disappointments were the failure to restore the University's reputation in astronomy, a subject that remained neglected, and the lack of funds for the further expansion of science before 1939. In Newcastle, applied science, the greatest strength of Armstrong College, became a faculty in its own right in 1928. At the College of Medicine the most notable development was in dental surgery, where degrees were introduced in 1925.

The UGC had wanted to see an even-handed expansion in Durham and encouraged the Council to strengthen the arts. Two eminent scholars, Alfred Guillaume and David Winton Thomas, laid the foundations of oriental studies. Guillaume later became Professor of Arabic at the University of London, while Winton Thomas left for Cambridge in 1938, where he took up the post of Regius Professor of Hebrew. Geography was introduced in 1928 when Gordon Manley was appointed as lecturer, later becoming senior lecturer and, ultimately, head of department before his departure in 1939. In Durham, he developed his reputation as an eminent climatologist. As curator of the Durham Observatory from 1931, he carried out his famous work on the Central England Temperature (CET) series, assembling monthly mean temperatures stretching back to 1659. In 1930 the history school was reorganised under Charles Whiting as professor. Durham's cash failed to stretch to the intended introduction of law. But economics flourished briefly under Laurence Helsby, a bright young Oxford graduate, who came to Durham in 1931. Helsby left Durham for the civil service in 1940, eventually heading the home civil service before his retirement with a peerage in 1968. Archaeology had been carried out through the Durham University Excavation Committee, formed in 1924 to provide practical experience for students in classics and history. Under Eric Birley, the subject became firmly established. Birley, with a double first from Oxford, came to the University in 1931 to lecture on Romano-British history and archaeology at both Newcastle and Durham. He was a world-renowned scholar on Hadrian's Wall and the Roman army, and worked tirelessly to promote archaeological

Eric Birley started excavating the famous Roman fort, Vindolanda, near Hadrian's Wall in the 1930s. Excavation continues today under the guidance of his son, Robin.

18 *Durham University Journal (DUJ),* 19 March 1966.
19 DUJ, 15 February 1963.

Durham students, 1951.

St Mary's rag float, 1948. St Mary's finally opened its doors to men in 2005.

By the 1930s a quarter of Durham students were women, they now account for over half the student population.

research in the north-east. Many of his archaeological finds from excavations can be seen in the Museum of Archaeology, now situated in the picturesque Old Fulling Mill. A dignified, warm and erudite individual, Birley would remain in Durham until his retirement in 1971, having established one of the leading university archaeological departments in the country.

About a quarter of the students were women by the 1930s. St Mary's had been recognised as a college in 1920, although there were still no new buildings. But there were many more women students than there were staff. By the early 1930s, Durham, unlike Newcastle, had not appointed any women as fellows. Women who did teach at the University often left once they were married, such as Dr Elsie Philips, Lecturer in Botany, who resigned her post at the end of the Easter term in 1928. Most of the women who came to study at Durham went into teaching. If they wished to pursue a lifetime in university teaching, they were expected to remain single; if they wished to marry and raise a family, they were expected to resign their posts.

Women students in Durham were still patronised, mainly by men, but also by other women. They were permitted to attend societies or clubs belonging to men's colleges only at the invitation of the head of the college concerned. In 1925, the Union Society in Newcastle opened its doors to women; in Durham, they remained firmly shut. This conservatism applied to the way in which women were treated by their own college. Miss Donaldson, the Principal of St Mary's from 1916 until 1940, strongly disapproved of her students meeting men without a chaperone. Breaches of the rules resulted in a summons to the Principal's study, where they were given a sound telling-off. Muriel Hood, a student there in the 1920s, recorded that the place was more like 'a strict boarding school'. The only way women seemed to be striking out on their own was on the river. The Durham Women Students' Association (DWSA) formed a boat club in 1926, and the first timed race between women crews took place in 1930, between the DWSA crew and another crew from Armstrong

St Hild's, 1965. The college amalgamated with St Bede's in 1975 .

College. In 1938 the Durham Colleges Women's Boat Club was founded, rowing before the war with success against teams from York and Newcastle.

Male students in Durham hardly enjoyed greater freedoms than women. They envied the situation in Newcastle, where men were allowed to entertain girlfriends in their rooms. John Mackereth, studying at Bede in the late 1920s, remembered that students were all confined to college after tea, except on half-days, when they were 'free' until 10 p.m. The men's colleges took as dim a view of relationships between male and female students as did the women's colleges. When Bede won the athletic sports competition one summer, a group of young men took the cups they had won onto the drive at St Hild's, the female teacher training college, and serenaded the girls, who leaned from their windows and shouted congratulations to them. The Principal of Bede, Evelyn Foley Braley, told his students that it was the blackest day in the history of the two colleges.

Sex was the unspoken fear of the college authorities, whose strict rules and regulations reflected the seriousness with which they took their quasi-parental responsibilities. In February 1918, as more mature students who had served at the front began to come up to Durham, it was agreed that a series of lectures on the risks of venereal disease should be given, separately, to both men and women. These lectures were repeated annually for several years.

Despite this, there was great fun to be had. In the late 1920s and early 1930s jazz was popular and students tripped the light fantastic to the music of the dance bands, such as Fred Lucas and his Syncopated Dance Band and the Original Rhythm Aces. The June ball was the highlight of June Week, although it depended on sponsors and donations as much as on ticket receipts, leading to complaints in the 1930s that too many free tickets were being handed out.

Angus MacFarlane-Grieve, Master of University College, a passionate advocate of the collegiate system.

It was said that the ball, like the rest of June Week, had become the plaything of 'the nouveau riche who class themselves as County'.[20]

Students could take part in rowing, cricket, rugby, soccer, hockey, tennis, fives, athletics and netball. Student sport at Durham was organised by the sports sub-committee of the Student Representative Council (SRC) until the Durham University Athletics Union (DUAU) was established in 1929. Two years later, DUAU became a full member of the Universities Athletics Union (UAU). The men's and women's swimming clubs were formed in 1931, and the golf and amateur boxing clubs in 1934.

At this time, most sport at Durham relied on the untiring commitment and enthusiasm of members of the University who gave their time willingly as amateur coaches. Rowing and rugby stand out between the wars. Until 1922 Colonel Lowe was the principal coach of the university boats. For many years afterwards this role was taken by Colonel Angus Macfarlane-Grieve. As a student at Durham he had been president of DUBC and had also played rugby for the University. He was among the small group of individuals whose interests – linking different parts of the University in Durham – kept the idea of an all-embracing collegiate institution alive. He was Censor, Bursar and eventually Master of University College; he was honorary treasurer of both DUBC and DUAU, as well as chairman of the Durham Regatta committee. The rising tide of rugby in Durham owed much to the organising ability of Hartley Elliott. He came to Durham as a student in 1929, took up secretarial responsibility for Durham Colleges' rugby and, in 1931, while still a student, joined the County Committee of the Rugby Football Union (RFU). Durham Colleges rugby gained the status of a senior county side and several players went on to play for the county. The calibre of the team was so good that one

Bede College football team, 1931.

20 'The History of June Week', in *Palatinate*, 17 June 1949.

Facing page, Durham has a long tradition of sporting excellence. A training run heading for St. Aidan's College.

Miner's Day Gala going up Saddler Street to the Cathedral – coal-mining reached a peak in the early 1920s with 170,000 men employed in the industry.

player, Jack Ellis, who later played for England in 1939, did not make the 1st XV.

Some progress was possible at the University during the depressed times of the early 1930s since the universities escaped largely unscathed from government spending cuts. The world on the University's doorstep, however, did suffer. It was impossible to ignore the plight and poverty of many of those thrown out of work from the mines, shipyards and engineering works. The antipathy of the bishop, the controversial Hensley Henson, towards the labour movement, despite his personal compassion, aroused strong feelings in Durham itself. The Dean, once mistaken for the Bishop, was thrown into the river. So when the centenary of the University came round in 1932, it was wisely and sensitively decided to postpone any celebrations. It was five years later when the University felt able to launch an anniversary appeal. During the 1930s the University completed a new block at Hatfield, new buildings on the science site and the expansion of the science site. But all this was only a small part of the plans repeatedly proposed in the early 1930s, which included a new women's college, improvements to other colleges, further extensions to the existing science buildings, the continued expansion of the library and a new

Union building. These had to wait for increased government grants, but as times began to improve, the universities (which had escaped cutbacks) had to wait for cuts in other public services to be restored before they could expect any more money.

In Newcastle, the College of Medicine concentrated on raising money to develop a completely new medical school on land next to Armstrong College. Under Sir Theodore Morison, who had the knack of attracting funding, Armstrong College embarked on an ambitious building programme. There were new departments, a library, a playing field and pavilion, and a students' union. In 1932, three years after Morison had been succeeded by Sir William Marris, came the opening of New Hall, the first men's hall of residence.

It was in Newcastle where the finely wrought 1908 constitution began to unravel. The crux of the matter was the exposure of just how powerless supposedly authoritative University bodies were in a time of crisis. In 1931 the Registrar, Sir Joseph Reed, and the Treasurer, Sir Robert Bolam, of the College of Medicine began the ruthless implementation of a new financial policy intended to secure the survival and future expansion of the college. But the cuts they imposed were savage; and the arbitrary way in which the college demanded the resignation of the Principal, without reference to the Senate, caused an outcry. They made the situation worse by abruptly terminating the arrangement with Armstrong College for medical students to receive tuition in chemistry, physics and biology. The incident caused uproar throughout the University and in Newcastle.

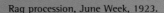

Rag procession, June Week, 1923.

The confidence of the public and the morale of staff and students were seriously damaged. There was no benefit to medical students, who were now confined to the outdated and overcrowded original college buildings. The arguments were so bitter that they soured relations between the two Newcastle colleges.[21]

The episode became a national issue and the chairman of the UGC called for action to resolve the situation. Ultimately, a Royal Commission was appointed under the chairmanship of former cabinet minister Lord Moyne. The remit of the Commission was wide-ranging: 'To enquire into the organization and work of the University of Durham and its constituent colleges and into the relation of the University to those colleges, and to report in what respects the present organization can be improved and what changes, if any, are desirable in the constitutions, functions and powers of the University and its constituent colleges.'[22] Since the origins of the crisis lay in Newcastle, perhaps it was not surprising that some of the strongest evidence in favour of radical reform came from Sir William Marris. He pointed out that the University lacked any independent corporate view and any powers to determine its own future development. The evidence from the Council of Durham Colleges was much more low-key, and expressed the view that the existing system was working well, stating that recent experience had 'revealed no vital defect in the constitution of the governing body and no reason for a grave break with tradition at the present time'.[23]

This was not the unanimous view of those in Durham. The commissioners were much more interested in a cogent and persuasive minority report in the names of Irvine Masson, Arthur Holmes and William Naysmith Smith of Durham County Council. They believed that the growth of the University had made its current administrative arrangements in Durham outmoded. Their report recommended that 'the functions of management – academic, financial and administrative – which at present are merged together in the hands of Council should be re-distributed'[24]. In particular, they hoped that this would at last provide staff with the opportunities to pursue original research that had been largely sacrificed in the effort to revive the University in the post-war period.

The commissioners issued their report in February 1935. They expressed the hope that Durham 'should have a future surpassing in dignity and usefulness anything which it has achieved in the past',[25] but they believed this could not be done without overhauling the way Durham was governed. The commissioners made a series of sweeping recommendations for change. The University would be governed by a small Court, made up of internal and external representatives, dealing with policy, finance and property matters, and by a strengthened Senate. Convocation's veto was finally abolished and all UGC funding would be channelled through the University. A University secretariat was formed, with offices in both Durham and Newcastle. All academic appointments would now be the responsibility of the University rather than the divisions. The Durham and Newcastle divisions would each be run by a council with a lay majority, responsible for property, finance and general administration, while academic boards became responsible for academic matters. Permanent heads would be appointed to run each division. In Durham the post of Warden was revived, while in Newcastle the post of Rector was created, each serving continuously, in turn, as Vice-Chancellor or Pro-Vice-Chancellor. The commissioners were understandably critical of the management of the College of Medicine. They considered, but rejected, the idea of creating a separate university in Newcastle. Instead, the two existing colleges would be merged into one. The Commission suggested the new college should be called University College, Newcastle. The Durham colleges successfully resisted this idea and instead it became King's College.

The proposals were largely supported by all sides and translated into the University of Durham Act, 1937. The new Council of Durham Colleges was appointed on 15 October 1937. The Dean and Chapter appointed two members, the Chancellor six and the county council four. Through the academic board the three heads of colleges (University, Hatfield and St Mary's), plus three other academic representatives, were also appointed to the Council. A similar change took place in Newcastle. 'Where there had been four incomplete and unclear systems arbitrarily formed and unclearly related, there were now three interlocking ones rationally devised in which there was a strong elective element to enable academic opinion to be expressed at all levels.'[26] The only flaw in this logic was that the University was ultimately led by a rotating double act that still had greater allegiance to each of the divisions than to the University as a whole. As it turned out, this was a strength.

In medieval times Durham Cathedral was a haven for criminals seeking sanctuary. A criminal would bang the sanctuary knocker at the north door on Palace Green to alert one of the watchmen. They were admitted into the cathedral, and offered sanctuary. They had to confess their crime to the coroner, and wear a black robe with a yellow cross on the shoulder. After 37 days of being looked after at the expense of the church, they had to leave the country by an assigned port. If they failed to comply, or deviated from the King's highway en route, they were executed.

21 See Bettenson, E M, 'The Great Divide', DUJ, 80, 1988.
22 *Royal Commission on the University of Durham Report*, HMSO, Cmd 4815, February 1935.
23 *Memorandum of Evidence for the Royal Commission on the University of Durham*, Durham, n.d., p. 17.
24 *Memorandum of Evidence*, pp. 20–1.
25 *Memorandum of Evidence*, p. 16.
26 Bettenson, 'The Great Divide', p. 178.

From Vision to Reality: 1937–63

O VER THE NEXT QUARTER OF A CENTURY, as higher education underwent momentous change, the reforms of the Royal Commission accomplished two seemingly contrary objectives. First, they held together the University of Durham – there were very few instances when Court or Senate disagreed along divisional lines. Second, they propelled each division along the path towards separation and independence.

Much of the credit for this achievement lies with two men whose close working partnership over the next fifteen years enhanced the University as a whole and the Durham and Newcastle divisions in particular. They came to the University in 1937 with a double advantage – while both men had links with Durham and Newcastle, they had been away long enough to enjoy the perspective of the outsider. They deserve to be recognised as the founders of the modern universities of Durham and Newcastle.

The new Warden of the Durham Colleges was James Duff. Born in Cambridge in 1898, he came from a Scots-Irish background. His father, J T Duff, a distinguished classics scholar, was a Fellow of Trinity College, Cambridge. Educated at Winchester, Duff served with the Royal Flying Corps in the First World War. His service ended after injuries sustained when he crash-landed his plane in 1917. Two years later he took up a scholarship at his father's college, where he studied classics and economics. In 1922 he became Assistant Lec-

The best short cut; Kingsgate Bridge spans the River Wear from New Elvet to South Bailey, linking University buildings on both sides of the river.

The legend of the the Dun Cow and the milkmaid is depicted in an 18th century carving on Durham Cathedral. Fleeing Viking raiders in the 9th century with the remains of St Cuthbert, his followers were directed in a vision to Dun Holm. After a fruitless search they overheard a milkmaid being told that her lost cow had been seen at Dun Holm. The overjoyed monks followed the milkmaid and established the cathedral and city of Durham there.

turer in Classics at Manchester University, before moving to Armstrong College in 1923 as Lecturer in Education. This was the subject closest to his heart. He was seconded to Northumberland county council as an educational superintendent, carrying out pioneering work on intelligence testing, before returning to Manchester in 1927 as Senior Lecturer in Education. Five years later, at the age of thirty-four, he was appointed professor. Apparently he was offered the post of Warden in 1937, on the recommendation of Sir Walter Moberly, chairman of the UGC and a former Vice-Chancellor of Manchester. Duff, who was knighted in 1950, stayed until his retirement in 1960.

James Duff, Warden of the Durham Colleges 1937–60, credited with laying the foundations of the modern University.

Duff looked like the man he was: in private, warm, witty and good company; in public, a grave and dignified presence as both head of the division and the alternating head of the University. He was a captivating conversationalist and a talented public speaker, with a ready command of language. At Manchester he was an outstanding public orator, and he created and then filled the same role at Durham. He never learned to drive, relying on chauffeurs, but his plane accident did not put him off flying. He worked best from noon onwards and quite happily carried on until the early hours of the next morning, a habit which did not endear him to W S Angus, the Registrar of the reformed University.

As an educationist, he was seen as being 'a progressive conservative',[27] an almost ideal quality for his post in Durham, where tradition required respect in the pursuit of change and expansion. He appreciated his good fortune in coming to Durham, which he loved, and was fond of quoting to freshers verse six of the sixteenth Psalm: 'The lines are fallen unto me in pleasant places – yea, I have a goodly heritage'.[28] Yet while he valued this heritage, he understood that Durham had to start turning itself into part of a viable modern university. Duff was particularly aware that Durham had always been apart from, rather than part of the community in which it was set. He wrote to his family before taking up the post that 'there is a certain air of spiritual mildew about Durham, with a strong clerical flavour that goes ill with the sort of University that a local University in an industrial area should aim at being'.[29] He did not make himself popular in Durham when he stifled the self-congratulation that student numbers had reached 500. Durham was not alone in being small, but Duff appreciated that its size, coupled with the heavy burden of tradition, threatened the division with ossification. As he pointed out to the Council within a few years of becoming Warden, 'we have not the special prestige of Oxford or Cambridge and we

have much scantier facilities . . . we can train for much fewer careers than any of the civic universities or colleges. Our one and only special line has been theology; and even in the interests of theological students themselves, a wider variety of other students is essential if Durham is to be a University in the full and literal sense of the word'.[30] For Duff, a small university was a contradiction in terms, since it could never attempt to be universal. While he was always a passionate supporter of the collegiate system, he also recognised that the cost of maintaining colleges for so few had been 'the rock on which pre-war Durham was continually in danger of foundering'.[31] He knew there were those who criticised him for 'thinking too much in terms of size', but he was unapologetic.[32]

Duff's partner in this duumvirate was the impeccably aristocratic Tory Lord Eustace Percy. Born in 1887, Percy was the seventh son and the twelfth of the thirteen children of the seventh duke of Northumberland. School at Eton was followed by a first class degree in modern history at Christ Church, Oxford. In 1909 Percy joined the diplomatic service, spending four years in Washington, DC from 1910. With a reputation as an American expert he was sent to Washington several times during the First World War. After contributing towards the creation of the League of Nations, he entered politics. He became the Conservative MP for Hastings in 1921 and quickly made his mark. In 1924, at the early age of 37, he entered the cabinet as president of the Board of Education. But he found himself falling between two stools, his progressive educational ideas resented by others in the party and opposed by the Treasury on the grounds of cost, forcing him to trim his sails. This, combined with his naturally imperious personality, meant that he was out of office from 1929 until 1935. In the meantime, he reinforced through his writings his reputation as a moderniser in education and other fields. This brought him back to the cabinet as minister without portfolio, a position without responsibility which he hated. Instead, he turned his back on national politics by resigning his seat in 1937 to become the first Rector of King's College.

Percy was a very different personality to Duff. He was naturally at ease with those in powerful and influential positions in a way that Duff never was. Often distant and aloof, he was born with a superior air that could irk others. But throughout his life his aristocratic instincts kept clashing with his democratic convictions. Roy Niblett, Deputy Registrar and then acting Registrar for most of the Second World War, recalled how Percy, inexperienced in academic life, wanted to foster closer links with students. He politely

27 Quoted in Batho, G R, 'Sir James Duff', in the *Oxford Dictionary of National Biography (ODNB)*, Oxford, 2004.
28 Quoted in Hird, M (ed.), *St Mary's College 1899–1974*, Durham, 1974.
29 Quoted in Batho, ODNB.

30 Quoted in the *Warden's Annual Report (WAR)* 1940–41, inserted with CDC minutes, 28 October 1941–24 November 1941.
31 *General Memo for the UGC*, n.d., in CDC minutes, 3 October 1950–19 July 1951.
32 *WAR* 1940–41.

requested his staff to send freshmen to see him whenever possible; he would, he said, try to calm any nerves on their part by attaching a welcoming notice on the outside of his study door. The notice, however, simply read, 'Do Not Knock. Come In'. This was an age when there was deep deference to authority, and the common reaction to this notice from a young student in his first term was puzzlement, followed by a gentle knock which, gaining no response, was repeated more loudly two or three times. Only then did the student pluck up courage to open the door slowly. Unfortunately, Percy hated having his explicit orders disobeyed and was at boiling point by this time. So when the student finally peered into the room, his welcome from the Rector consisted of a furious admonition for failing to pay heed to a simple notice.

Friedrich Paneth, Professor of Chemistry, 1939–53, known for achievements in inorganic and analytical chemistry. A pioneer of radiochemistry and founder of a new discipline, cosmochemistry.

Yet the differences between the two men disguised their similarities. They had in common integrity and intellectual ability. They both possessed abundant energy, even though Percy preferred to start his working day early in the morning and continue until the early evening. Educationally, they were both in the same camp. From their different backgrounds and experiences they both respected tradition but favoured progress. It was equally true to say of Duff, as it was of Percy, that he was 'a dreamer of dreams who was at the same time a man of action'.[33] They learned to put up with each other's foibles – Percy with Duff's perverse working hours, Duff with Percy's often infuriating nitpicking over detail. Disagreements came over matters of principle. These could be fierce, but were held openly and honestly. And, remarks Niblett, 'when he had resolutely made up his mind, Duff could and usually did win these'.[34]

As both men settled into their roles and began building the relationship that proved to be so vital, the University Court announced a public appeal to raise £350,000 (approximately £15 million today). Durham's priorities remained the implementation of the plans for St Mary's College, the further development of the science site and a new students' union, estimated to cost about £110,000 in total. The appeal made slow progress and by early 1939 only £115,000 had been raised. Consent was given for Durham to proceed with the science laboratories and the new union. At the same time, the Castle Preservation Fund Committee, having at last completed the restoration of the building, handed it back to the Council of Durham Colleges. In Newcastle, the new medical school, completed in 1938, was opened in the following year by King George VI. One of Duff's earliest innovations, achieved in 1938, was the creation of boards of studies for individual subjects. Until then, teaching staff had been employed directly by the Council. For the first time, arts subjects were given a departmental focus. Numbers in Newcastle reached more than 1500, but in Durham, because of a cutback in teacher training places, they dropped to the low 400s, underlining Duff's view on the importance of size. But any plans for expansion and development harboured by Duff in Durham and Percy in Newcastle were scuppered in September 1939 by the beginning of another world war.

Buildings in progress ground to a halt, buildings planned were postponed and new appointments were deferred as post-holders were called up. Among the last were the new Professors of Greek and Classical Literature and, a little later, of Hebrew and Oriental Languages. The former, who never returned to Durham, was the twenty-seven-year-old Enoch Powell, already a professor, later a government minister and controversial Conservative MP; the latter was Thomas Thacker, himself only twenty-eight at the outbreak of war, who had come as Reader in Hebrew in 1938. Thacker would return and make a significant contribution to enhancing the scholarly reputation of the University.

There was one member of staff whom the University was more than happy to keep. Dr Friedrich Paneth, a brilliant inorganic chemist and expert in radioactivity, had decided to stay in Britain after the Nazis came to power in Germany in 1933. He became Reader in Atomic Chemistry at the University of London and was invited to take up the chair in chemistry at Durham in 1939, following Masson's departure. As an Austrian exile, Paneth was in danger of being interned at the start of the war. Instead he became a naturalised British citizen and remained Professor of Chemistry at Durham until 1953. He was absent from Durham for two years during the war when he was sent to be head of the chemistry division of the joint British-Canadian Atomic Energy Laboratory in Montreal. Elected a Fellow of the Royal Society in 1947, he perpetuated and strengthened the reputation of chemistry in Durham. Another exile who came directly to Durham was Wilhelm Levison, an eminent medieval historian ejected from his professorship in Germany by the Nazis because he was Jewish. Bertram Colgrave, Reader in English at Durham, knew Levison, and was instrumental in persuading the University authorities to offer him a post. They agreed, even though there was no money for it, and Levison spent his final years as an academic in Durham.

The war affected Newcastle less than it did Durham. Plans

33 DUJ, 12 May 1958.
34 Niblett, R, 'Reminiscences', in *Durham First*, Autumn 2000.

RAF cadets came to Durham in World War II to study maths, physics and electronics. Passing out parade, 1942.

Durham in wartime. In 1941 the first of a steady flow of young cadets began to stream into the University, those from the artillery heading for Newcastle, those from the RAF for Durham. They came to study mainly maths, physics and mechanics, condensing the first year of an undergraduate course into six months. This was extremely innovative at the time and Durham's quick response to the nation's needs was commendable. The newly created state bursaries also brought more talented students to study science in Durham. These extra numbers – there were 323 students in late 1941 – invigorated Durham. The creation of the University Air Squadron alongside the Officer Training Corps helped to bridge the increasingly apparent divide between students in Durham and those in Newcastle. One King's College student, Guy Oddie, remembered that for many Newcastle students, Durham before the war was no more than a small town with a cathedral, a miners' gala and, some said, a population dominated by 'parsons, publicans and prostitutes'.[35]

Ken Hoyle was one of the RAF trainee aircrew selected to go up to Durham. He remembered how students allocated dingy rooms on the North Bailey at first envied those singled out for sets of rooms in the castle with their views of Framwellgate. But the latter soon discovered that the 10.30 p.m. curfew turned their palace into a prison. It was much

RAF cadets dining at the Castle in World War II.

to evacuate most students and staff to Durham were abandoned very quickly. Newcastle lost staff and students to war service, but with far fewer students to start with, Durham's loss was much more serious. 'Makeshift and economy have to prevail in all directions', wrote Duff in his annual report for 1939–40. Money was saved by not replacing staff, but a full curriculum was maintained with the help of King's College. By the end of 1940 there were 270 students in Durham. June Week was abandoned, games were curtailed. Hatfield College was leased to the county council to house the displaced Neville's Cross teacher training college, while the remaining Hatfield students were sent across to University College for the rest of the war. Students from Bede College were transferred to York in order to accommodate students evacuated from London. Duff worried that Durham certainly, the University perhaps, would have to close if the war continued much longer. Durham, he lamented, was suffering because of a lack of the vocational subjects that provided students with military exemption.

But the government, learning the lessons from the First World War, made better use of the universities in the Second. It was not surprising that the favoured universities were those with a reputation for science. The exceptional work of those early science pioneers like Masson, Holmes and Wagstaff, in the 1920s and 1930s, helped to save

35 *Durham First*, Autumn 1994.

easier to escape from the North Bailey for a rendezvous with 'friendly young ladies'. After the war, Hoyle was among the fifth of his comrades who returned to complete their degrees in 1946–47. Some though, after their experience of war, found it impossible to settle back into a student lifestyle and about a third dropped out.[36]

The women students provided a continuity lacking when so few men other than chemists or physicists stayed longer than a year. Many of them had vivid memories of wartime in Durham. Before the war, when so many women struggled to finance their studies, even laddering one's stockings could prove a financial embarrassment. One of the few blessings of wartime, remembered Helen Hudson from St Mary's, was how clothes rationing disguised this poverty. Rationing imposed other stringencies too, as the Assistant Bursar of the college, Betty Booth, recalled. These were years when baskets full of rabbits were brought back from the Saturday markets, when it was hard to persuade the greengrocer to allow one banana per head, when all sorts of ways were valiantly tried to make whale meat palatable.[37]

The war was bringing to the universities men and women for whom such a destination might have seemed unthinkable before the war. This development began to generate new thinking about the future of universities once peace returned. This was part of the strengthening mood for social change in a nation that had emerged exhausted from a depression, only to be ground down again during the hardship of war. The stagnant state of higher education some had complained about before the war was being stirred up. Writers like Bruce Truscott, social reformers like Sir Ernest Simon, organisations like the Association of Scientific Workers and the Association of University Teachers, all wanted to see an expanded and more generously funded university system. Reports published during and shortly after the war, such as the McNair Report, the Percy Report and the Barlow Report, also envisaged an enhanced role for the universities. In 1943 the UGC itself surveyed the universities about their post-war needs and aspirations. The following year, the Butler Education Act, in completely reforming the system of primary and secondary education, replaced the arbitrary scholarship route to university with more systematic selection, although this came only through the grammar and public schools. There was an emphasis on equality of opportunity, although this was never quite fulfilled.

In this spirit, despite many other pressing priorities at a time of economic austerity, the Labour government elected in 1945 agreed to fund the capital expenditure required for the expansion of the universities for the decade after 1947. Like other decisions made by the new government, this was an act of vision, taken at a most difficult time, that had huge national benefits in the long term. The UGC invited the Committee of Vice-Chancellors and Principals (CVCP) to

forecast an increase in the number of students for the same period. The Durham and Newcastle divisions submitted separate estimates to the UGC in the autumn of 1945. The Newcastle submission noted that with 1,700 students the capacity of the existing city centre site had been reached, although the proposals of the city council for a new site would cater for almost infinite growth. But any expansion in numbers could come only by widening what had been predominantly a local catchment area before the war. Newcastle was not alone in making this break. The change in grants after the war to cover residential costs began to sever the link between many civic universities and their immediate areas by attracting students from further away. In Durham's case, of course, anything that made coming to a residential university easier was an advantage. This was also helped by the Ministry of Education's recognition for the first time, in 1947, that college fees should cover supervision and tuition as well as maintenance. Newcastle's paper also made the point that if more students came to King's College, the arts departments would have to be expanded and student accommodation increased.

The submission on behalf of the Durham colleges was permeated by the arguments that James Duff had been making ever since his arrival. Durham was too small in every respect – in its colleges, its departments and the number of staff – risking isolation and in danger of becoming too narrow. But Duff stressed that it was impossible to expand student numbers without a programme of new building, and by that he was looking beyond the completion of St Mary's. For Duff, any growth had to be under the control of the Council, which was still responsible only for three of the division's eight colleges. If funding could be found, Duff maintained, there was plenty of land available south of the river, close to the science site. He believed that only once the problem of residential accommodation had been solved would it be possible to tackle other areas. This was a common problem for almost every university, but Duff, passionately committed to Durham, was acutely aware that the next ten years would be critical. 'For more than a century it has been prophesied that Durham should become a great residential University of the North, and for more than a century the prophecy has so conspicuously failed to come true that we ourselves are most reluctant to repeat it. Yet it could come true . . . It cannot happen in a decade, and yet the next decade may well decide whether it is to happen or not.[38]' He was absolutely right.

If new colleges were built, Duff believed that Durham could double in size within ten years, from 500 to more than 1,000 students. Durham, he said, had to be a residential university out of choice and necessity. Pressed by the UGC in the summer of 1946, following their visit to the University, he agreed to increase this estimate to a maximum of 2,000,

36 See *Durham First*, Spring 2000.
37 See Hird.
38 *Estimate of the Expansion of the University*, CDC minutes, 30 Oct. 1945.

Facing page, relaxing beneath a blossoming tree at St Mary's College.

St Mary's College was founded in 1919 having started life as the Women's Hostel in 1899. It moved to this, its current site, in 1952.

Princess Elizabeth laid the foundation stone for St Mary's College at the start of building work, 1947.

Grey College, founded in 1959, was named after the second Earl Grey, a keen supporter of the University in the 19th century.

although he felt this would lead to growing tension with the Newcastle division, which was forecast to reach 3,000 students. If Durham grew, it would have to teach subjects currently taught only in Newcastle.

Over the next few years the UGC did its best to fulfil Duff's dream. Every request for capital funding was met. Yet it took five years to complete St Mary's after the foundation stone was laid by Princess Elizabeth in 1947. This was nothing compared to the gestation of the new men's college. Approved by the University in 1947, it was ten years before work started and fourteen years before it opened. Lumley Castle, leased to the University by Lord Scarbrough in 1945, was seen as temporary accommodation for students at University College, but remained in use until 1970. A small block was added to Hatfield College, but that replaced existing inadequate accommodation. Shincliffe Hall was used to house the growing number of women belonging to St Aidan's Society, as the Home Students were renamed, but there was constant pressure from the Principal, Miss Ethleen Scott, to turn the Society into a college, complete with new buildings. St Cuthbert's Society was also badly in need of premises. As for the handful of married students in the division, there was no official provision at all. One couple complained in early 1949 that they were living in a caravan.

What had happened? This was still a period of national economic hardship. Building controls were not finally removed until 1955. Materials and labour were not always easy to procure. Grants were scaled back as the UGC could not cope with the demands from universities, which were taken aback by their increased popularity after the war.[39] James Duff noted in 1950 that Durham had miscalculated the grants it would need, since 'we badly underestimated the rate at which our numbers would increase after the war'. There had been a failure to appreciate how easily Durham would absorb another 400 students and how easily students would obtain full grants for their studies. By the autumn of 1948, there were already nearly 1,100 students resident in Durham. The result was that departments had their hands full, residential accommodation was bulging and there were more than 400 students without college accommodation. Nothing much changed for the next ten years. To make sure students were properly housed, a lodgings officer was appointed. Tom Gardiner, attending Durham in the 1950s, recalled that lodg-

39 Memorandum to 39 UGC, October 1950, in CDC minutes, 3 October 1950–19 July 1951.

ings could be found in Durham for £2 10s a week, all in, with bathroom. 'That was more than King's could offer in Newcastle. A friend of mine with lodgings in Gateshead had his set bath night in front of the living room fire, and all the marriageable daughters managed to barge in and look him over.'[40]

With 3,212 students, the Newcastle division was in the same situation. As Duff had predicted, tensions were creeping into the relationship between the two divisions. In 1947 Percy, as Vice-Chancellor, wrote that the 1937 constitution was creaking under the strain of the University's rapid post-war growth. The University as a body was as ineffective now as it had become under the 1910 constitution. The two divisions were acting as de facto universities and the University could do nothing other than continue to delegate a large part of its responsibilities to both of them. Newcastle, he wrote, would sooner or later claim independent university status and should be treated as one until that happened. Not to do so would only create mounting discontent. In some of his proposals, Percy was actually advocating a return to the status quo before 1937 that had proved so divisive. His ultimate proposal was to change the name of the University to the University of Durham and Newcastle, with each division becoming respectively the University of Durham and the University of Newcastle. The Warden and the Rector would become Vice-Chancellors.

The body representing academic staff in the Durham colleges resisted this solution, but was realistic about the long-term outcome. The Academic Board of the Durham Colleges noted that 'there is no real choice in the other direction, namely away from central control, except a quite definite parting of the ways into two Universities'.[41] But such a split had to be planned and phased in to give the Durham colleges time to create the broader curriculum needed to sustain Durham as an independent university. Until then, any weakening of the existing arrangements should be resisted.

On St Valentine's Day 1950, a conference held on the reconstitution of the University recommended that no objection should be made to Newcastle's application to become a separate university. The University Court at once began to stall. The Court invited its chairman, Lord Scarbrough, and vice-chairman, Dr Edward Collingwood, to report on the future of the University, but only after making quite clear its unhappiness with the idea of separation. It seems likely that Duff and Percy did not see eye to eye over this issue. Percy was obviously pressing for separation; Duff never had any objection to separation, but his ambition had always

George Macaulay Trevelyan, eminent historian, being welcomed by university staff and students at Durham Station on his way to his installation as Chancellor, 1950.

been to ensure that the Durham colleges on their own were strong enough for independence before that happened. Duff clearly believed that the right time had not yet arrived. One wonders whether his hand can be seen in the Court's response.

The conclusion of the Scarbrough Report was not a surprise. It was lukewarm at best about separation, and instead struck out, in disregard of the evidence, in favour of continued cooperation to create a single outstanding university. Its only sop to Newcastle was approval of the change of name recommended by Percy, but in the event this proved so unpopular with Convocation that it was never implemented. But Duff's agenda was furthered by recommendations that Durham should expand into territory previously the preserve of Newcastle, including applied science and law, so that it might be able to flourish independently at some time in the future. For Percy, whose contribution to the progress of both divisions and the University as a whole had proved invaluable, the Scarbrough Report was a sign that it was time to go. Under his leadership, the future of Newcastle as an independent university had become almost inevitable. Student and staff numbers had increased, departments and chairs had multiplied, a new site was planned and developed, with new blocks for science, civil engineering and the arts, new residential blocks and an extended library. Percy retired in 1952 and was succeeded as Rector by Dr Charles Bosanquet. Sadly, Percy died in 1958 and so failed to see Newcastle become a university in its own right.

Many of the students whose mass precipitated this constitutional crisis were ex-servicemen, with a handful of ex-servicewomen. According to one student, they brought Durham back to life after a period when the colleges had been 'devoid of all student activity and when the Union was a defunct and decrepit pile'.[42] With their wartime experience, these mature students,

Front cover of the Rag magazine, 1951.

40 *Durham First*, Autumn 1997.
41 Senate minutes, 18 May 1948.
42 *Palatinate*, 10 November 1950.

mixing with those straight from school, created a distinct atmosphere in the city during the late 1940s and early 1950s. Adults already, unlike most of Durham's students, who were still minors, they had lived fuller lives before coming to college than many of their younger peers would after graduating. A student could discover, quite by chance, that he might well be sitting next to the holder of a Distinguished Flying Cross and bar, although he would never tell you himself. Instinctively chafing against many of the rules and regulations, especially the continuing requirement to wear gowns for much of the time, their less deferential approach was one of the first signs of a changing attitude in students towards authority. In their more confident relationships with staff, this was something the Warden entirely approved of, rather than the stiffness and shyness that he had found to be prevalent before the war. It also helped, of course, that many of the staff were not much older than their students.

The atmosphere these newcomers created was described in a number of articles in *Palatinate*, the newly founded student newspaper. The ex-servicemen dazzled young women with their wartime stories, service glamour, money and even, sometimes, a car. The result was that some women found themselves succumbing 'to advanced techniques which in the normal run of things they would not have encountered until they were at least five years older'[43]. Other women, however, were often appalled by the way many men looked them up and down as if they were cattle, commenting inanely to each other and guffawing loudly. One article painted a picture of the appearance of the typical male in the late 1940s, where 'the affectation of the corduroy trousers, the mammoth brogues, Joseph's coats and exotic cigarette-holders is only balanced by the exhibitionist display of ex-officer trousers, macks and greatcoats'.[44]

By 1950 almost all the older servicemen had passed through Durham, but most of the new male students were arriving after completing two years' national service. Durham was revitalised by this mixture of men and women. For one thing, the rise in numbers strengthened the college system, as Duff had known it would. More students in larger colleges injected vigour into the life of the Durham division. The colleges were producing better sport, music, drama, journalism and debating. By 1948 two-thirds of the students in Durham belonged to colleges controlled by the Council. In the previous year the non-collegiate societies had been reorganised, with their own governing bodies and Principals. Bede became a full college within the division and began accepting undergraduates other than trainee teachers. Although there remained a gulf between the teacher-training students and the undergraduates, this was attributed to 'the growing independence of the certificate [training] colleges and a mixture of ignorance and snobbery from the university'.[45] The trainee teacher did not wear a gown, was not a member of the Union, was ineligible to play games for the University (as opposed to the Durham Colleges) and had no representation on the SRC. Greater numbers of students also helped Hatfield College, which at one time had looked likely to be absorbed

43 *Palatinate*, 28 May 1948.
44 *Palatinate*, 17 March 1948.
45 *Palatinate*, 28 May 1948.

The women's team is among the best in the country. Cricket was first played at the University in 1843 and the men's team has won the university championship title 10 times since 1991.

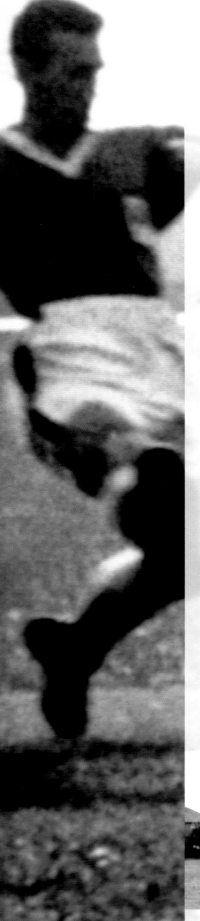

entirely by University College because of low numbers. Instead, Hatfield regained its independence in 1949, under Eric Birley as Master. Hatfield was the first college to create tutorial groups under resident tutors, a system of academic and pastoral guidance that was introduced successfully throughout the other colleges. Duff also ensured that Durham's claim to be residential and collegiate meant something to most staff, by making sure any new appointments were attached either to a college or a society through membership of the senior common room.

There was a wide range of sporting activity. College teams played each other and the Durham Colleges played King's College and the Medicals, as they were known. Standards in rowing, for so long the premier sport, improved dramatically. In 1949 Durham competed for the first time in an eight-oared event at the Head of the River on the Thames, and by the following year was described as the strongest club in the north. The president of the Durham Colleges Athletics Union reported in 1949 that almost every student in Durham took part in some kind of sport. But the sudden rise in student numbers made decent playing fields essential. In May 1951 work began on laying out sports fields on thirteen and a half acres at Maiden Castle, on the way out of Durham, towards Shincliffe.

The University was already producing a handful of sporting stars. Warren Bradley, a student at Hatfield, captained the soccer team at Durham in 1953–54, went on to play for Manchester United between 1958 and 1962, and gained eleven amateur international caps and three full England caps. Then there was Frank Tyson, one of the great international cricketers of all time. Tyson too was a student at Hatfield, the sports editor of

Palatinate, with his own column, 'Frankly Speaking', and a member of the Durham Colleges and University cricket teams. News had got round about his precocious talent soon after Tyson arrived in Durham. The captain of the University cricket team in 1950, Donald Heaton, decided to go and watch him play for the Durham Colleges against King's College. 'I had never before seen field placing like it. I walked to the boundary and it was time for the fifth over. The bowler in question had a silly mid-on and a silly mid-off, three slips, one gulley (fine), two leg slips and, I have to say it, a long stop. The slips were halfway to the boundary. The third ball of this particular over took off from a good length and hit the sight screen without bouncing. The scorer credited a "six" bye which we got him to amend to "four". Durham Colleges won.'[46] The demon bowler was Tyson, who was immediately invited to join the University side.

The University 1st XI won the UAU cricket championship in Tyson's last year, 1953. In the previous year the University had also won the rugby championship, a feat repeated in 1955. John Rogers, who played rugby for University College, the Durham Colleges and the University in the late 1940s, recalled that there were no training sessions, just a Wednesday afternoon practice before every Saturday match. 'We were a puny bunch (I was seventeen when I went up to Durham and weighed about eleven stone – and I was a forward). The local teams frequently included fifteen stone miners. I was grateful on one occasion to hear the opposition's captain say to his forwards, "Go easy, lads, they're only students".'[47]

But the opportunity for the University to make its mark on the wider sporting scene also exposed the weaknesses of an organisation split into two halves. The

Warren Bradley, *main picture, and below,* captained the Durham University soccer team in the early 1950s, and went on to play for Manchester United and England.

Frank Tyson studied English Literature at Hatfield College, 1950–55. A legendary fast bowler known as 'Typhoon Tyson', he became a national hero as part of the winning Ashes team in 1954–55. Tyson believes that he bowled his fastest for the University XI which won the Universities Athletic Union Championship in 1953.

46 *Durham First*, Spring 2000.
47 *Durham First*, Spring 2004.

Graeme Fowler, cricket coach, third right, Frank Tyson, second right, with members of Durham University Cricket Club (DUCC), 1999.

A scene from *Bacchae* by Euripides staged in 2003. Durham's Dramatic Society dates from 1934.

distance between Durham and Newcastle made it difficult to create cohesive and effective University teams. Many students saw playing for the Durham Colleges', King's or Medicals' sides as more important than representing the University. 'There is,' wrote one student, 'much greater delight in our defeating Newcastle at sport than there is in a victory by the University side.'[48]

Other activities were also based on the divisions rather than the University. In Durham, the focus for drama was the Durham Colleges Dramatic Society (DCDS), founded in 1934, supplemented by the college dramatic societies. In 1950 DCDS finally found a home in the converted, though still inadequate, Assembly Rooms. There was a Durham Colleges Orchestra and a Durham Colleges Choral Society. A lot of this was thanks to the commitment of the Lecturer in music, Peter Evans. Before he left in 1963 to become Southampton University's first Professor of Music, he had also founded the highly regarded Palatine Opera Group and had become a respected critic of contemporary avant-garde music.

Palatinate was supposed to be the University newspaper. It was started in 1948 by Les George, a twenty-six-year-old ex-serviceman studying at Bede, with fellow student Peter Kaufman, who also acted as sports correspondent. But covering both divisions of the University proved impractical and Newcastle eventually went its own way. This too heightened the tension between the two divisions, as rival student journalists took potshots at each other. The fortunes and standards of *Palatinate* fluctuated over the years, but it provided an invaluable training ground for several future stars of British journalism, including Harold Evans (editor, 1951–52), Hunter Davies (editor, 1956–57), Judith Hann (editor, 1962–63), George Alagiah (editor, 1976–77) and Jeremy Vine (editor, 1985–86).

With more students, there were many clubs, devoted to a whole host of interests, from contract bridge and mathematics, exploration and natural history, music and history, religion and languages to the Labour Club and the Conservative and Unionist Association. Durham also had a Communist Society, although it was wound up in 1954.

The political climate in Durham in the late 1940s and early 1950s was dominated by the cold war. Student feeling, it was reported, 'is generally and in some cases violently anti-communist'. This applied equally to the University authorities. When the Warden refused to permit the Durham Colleges ice hockey team to attend the World University Games in Prague in 1949, it was on the grounds that foreign tours were forbidden during term-time. Howard Phelps, later president of the SRC and chairman of the University Council, represented the protests of the SRC to the Warden. He remembered how Duff was suspicious of a communist state, while students on the left saw it as a role model for the SRC. A second ban, two years later, on a visit to Rumania, killed off ice hockey. (One team member, Peter Woodcock, remembered that in the late 1940s there were three Norwegians and one Canadian in the team, which sported a home-made kit of woollen jerseys and padding pinched from cricket and football gear.) The Durham Colleges SRC was already flexing its post-war muscles, protesting against rises in

48 *Palatinate*, 3 June 1949.

PALATINATE

FORTNIGHTLY NEWSPAPER FOR DURHAM UNIVERSITY STUDENTS

No. 1   WEDNESDAY, MARCH 17th, 1948 · 2 NOV 1948   THREEPENCE

" How many goodly creatures are there here ! How beauteous mankind is ! O brave new world, That has such people in't ! "
Tempest.

These Men . . . !

I like men, but I frankly detest the undergraduate specimens. Insincere, affected, self assured and bombastic, they grate upon the very fibres of my feminine sensibilities.

From the woman's point of view, my first antipathy to male undergraduates finds its root, and a low root it is, in their calmly appraising glances. They look us up and down like cattle, they comment among themselves and then guffaw in unison. Would they dare to do the same to a man? Indeed not, for the male is a cowardly animal, and—caught on his own—rapidly changes his bombast for a sheepish and embarrassed grin.

This grin is often camouflaged, hidden by a permanent, revolting and unhygienic fungus. We watch the latter's expansionist policy with fascination, until finally we realise that the proud owner of the growth has been able to dispense with collar as well as chin.

Ladies—let us compare notes for a while. How many different types of approach have been made to you? Very few, I warrant! "How

Durham Rag Week 1948

Rag Week will take place during the week of May 3rd-8th instead of, as hitherto, at the end of the term. Last year it was felt that such things as June examinations interfered seriously with the carrying out of the various activities designed to empty the pockets of the Durham public. The new date has now the support of the Council of the Durham Colleges and it is hoped that the greater amount of time made available to students will result in really large scale participation by everyone.

One of the chief problems facing the Rag Committee and S.R.C. has been that of allocation of the proceeds. The impending nationalisation of the hospitals caused many people to feel that a disincentive to giving money to our traditional beneficiaries existed. For this reason the money that is made will be divided between a number of local charities selected by a sub-committee of S.R.C. and in addition some specific item of equipment will be purchased for the Durham County Hospital and which will be marked as a donation from the Colleges Rag Week

Harold Evans, editor, 1951/2.

George Alagiah editor, 1976/7.

Hunter Davies, editor, 1956/7.

Palatinate seller, Sophie Tuckwell,1990.

Wendy Pilmer, editor, 1985/6.

Background, the first edition of *Palatinate*, the student newspaper, 1948.

tuition and maintenance fees and fighting for representation on the Council of Durham Colleges. The idea of a student's rector was raised briefly in 1951, as a ruse to persuade the Warden to revive the previous custom of inviting the president of the SRC to meet him and the Council Secretary. But Durham was never a hotbed of radical politics, no matter how fervently some tried to raise the temperature, and the moderate views of most students were usually taken (not always correctly) as a sign of political apathy.

The rapid rise in Durham's student numbers came partly because of a concerted attempt to encourage more young men and women to study science at university. The Barlow Report in 1946 urged an overall expansion of universities in the UK through raising the proportion of science students and investing in the necessary teaching and research facilities. While total student numbers in England and Wales rose from 65,000 in 1947 to 90,000 in 1961, the proportion of science students increased from 26 per cent before the war to 34 per cent in 1954, and 41 per cent in 1961. In the early 1950s, Durham exceeded the national average, with more than 36 per cent of all students studying science in 1952–53. Duff was quick to use the official bias in favour of science to Durham's advantage. In 1945 the chemical giant ICI gave funds to support several new science fellowships for a period of seven years. Thanks to government sponsorship and the involvement of Professor Paneth, the Londonderry Radiochemistry Laboratory was opened by Lord Portal in 1947. This was important because it was designed to attract top quality researchers to Durham. Chairs in botany and zoology were created in 1950, fulfilling the ambition of those who had founded the science department a generation earlier of having five departments under individual professors. Work had started on the new building to house geography and mathematics on the science site. The West Building, with a science library and a new 300-seat lecture theatre, named the Applebey Theatre after the Council chairman, opened in May 1952. Science teaching and research accommodation in Durham had more than trebled since 1939, yet some laboratories would remain prefabricated huts until the 1990s.

Durham's ambitions in science were also signalled by several outstanding senior appointments made by Duff. In 1944 Lawrence Wager succeeded Arthur Holmes as Professor of Geology. Another brilliant geologist, Wager was elected a Fellow of the Royal Society in 1946, left Durham for Oxford in 1950 and was later knighted. His successor was equally outstanding. Kingsley Dunham had studied at Durham under Arthur Holmes. Dunham expanded the department, based on his own interest in the origin of economic mineral deposits, and enhanced its reputation. He was elected Fellow of the Royal Society in 1955 (he was not the first Durham graduate to be so honoured – Professors Hawkes, Westoll and Tolansky achieved that honour jointly in 1952) and remained at Durham until his appointment as director of the Institute of Geological Sciences in 1967. Knighted in 1972, he later returned to Durham as Professor Emeritus. In 1955, another Durham graduate succeeded John Wagstaff as Professor of Physics. After graduating with first class honours from Armstrong College, George Rochester had made a

Sir Kingsley Charles Dunham, was a Professor of Geology at the University from 1950–71 and held the post of Professor Emeritus. He is well known for his classic publication, *The Geology of the North Pennine Orefield.*

Department of Earth Sciences.

4 From Vision to Reality: 1937–63   63

Early Cosmic Ray research at the University using an 11-tonne electromagnet.

The Cosmic Ray Spectrum, Physics Department, 1964.

name for himself through the study of cosmic rays – research begun while he was at Manchester University from 1937 to 1955. He continued this work at Durham, creating national and international links with other universities at a time when Durham's academic horizons were generally limited. He brought to the department a host of other talented physicists. A J Apostolakis and J V Major concentrated on the study of particle accelerators. Arnold Wolfendale, later the Astronomer Royal, furthered Rochester's work on cosmic rays, reviving the study of astronomy at Durham. Rochester's tenure at Durham, thanks to his international reputation and his commitment to the department, laid the foundations for Durham's renown as one of the country's leading universities for physics. A modest man, Rochester was elected a Fellow of the Royal Society in 1958 and retired in 1973, widely regarded as the finest physicist never to have been awarded the Nobel prize.

Alongside the promotion of science in universities came the expansion of the social sciences, or, as they were known, social studies. When Duff was planning Durham's post-war future, this seemed an ideal way to recruit a wider range of students, including those who would not previously have considered coming to university. The new BA in social studies was first considered in 1943 and introduced in 1946. The BA in general studies, or general degree, was also introduced at the same time for the same reasons.

George Rochester, Professor of Physics and department Chair, 1955-73, Pro-Vice Chancellor from 1967-70. A founding figure of modern particle physics.

Professor Sir Arnold Wolfendale FRS is known internationally for his research into the origin and nature of the cosmic radiation. He is Emeritus Professor of Physics at Durham University and was Astronomer Royal, 1991–95.

High ambitions were held for the new department of social studies, even though at first it consisted of no more than one Lecturer in Politics and another in Economics. Francis Hood, who had lectured in economics and history at the University since 1922, was the first Professor of Political Theory and Institutions, created in 1945. Law was intended as part of the new department. There had been a law school at Newcastle since 1923, but the subject had not been taught at Durham since the 1870s. But there were so many other priorities within the division that, although a part-time Lecturer in Legal Theory was appointed at Michaelmas 1947, law became part of the social studies and general degrees only in 1959, while an honours school in the subject had to wait until 1966.

The social studies degree, in fact, did not prove as popular as the University had anticipated and the real expansion of the department did not occur until the 1960s. On the other hand, there was a huge demand for the general degree, both the new BA and the existing BSc. By the late 1940s this was creating a problem. An influx of ex-servicemen, without the qualifications to read for honours, studying for general or pass degrees, created too many large classes and an unacceptably high failure rate. This fuelled concerns about the quality of the general degree that persisted until it was abolished forty years later. But the general degree was important for Durham because it was taken by almost every student entering the University through the teacher training

Durham has one of the leading Mathematical Sciences departments in Britain.

$(x^2+y^4)dy^2-2xy\,dx\,dy+(-x^2+2y^2+y...$

The disc... has an... $X_{1/2}-S...$

Characteristic curves on a hyperbolic Whitney Umbrella

A Persian tile dating from the Qajar Dynasty, 1869-90 in the Oriental Museum. The museum's remarkable collection was started after the founding of the School of Oriental Studies by Professor T.W. Thacker in 1947. World famous, the collection consists of artefacts from the civilisations and cultures of Asia, Egypt, Islamic North Africa, the Near and Middle East.

colleges. This stemmed from the 1944 McNair Report, which had envisaged a completely graduate teaching profession. Durham was among the universities that became validation bodies for teacher training qualifications and established its own Institute of Education under Professor Stanley in 1947.

Alongside the creation of social studies after the war was the development of oriental studies under the energetic Professor Thacker. In 1945 a Foreign Office committee on the study of Oriental, Slavonic, East European and African languages invited the universities to suggest how they might become involved. The committee happened to be chaired by Lord Scarbrough, who already had close links with the Durham colleges, having offered the use of the family seat, Lumley Castle, to the University in 1944. The committee recommended in 1946 that a school of Near and Middle Eastern Studies should be established at a northern university. There was a debate over whether this should be in Manchester, where a nucleus for such studies already existed, or in Durham, where there was only Professor Thacker and his enthusiasm. Lord Scarbrough also happened to chair the committee allocating the funds and, with the wisdom of Solomon, divided the grant between Manchester and Durham. By the end of the 1940s, Durham's school of oriental studies, with six teaching staff, offered courses in Hebrew, Arabic, Ancient Egyptian, Coptic, Assyrian, Persian and comparative Semitic philology. The degree in oriental studies was introduced in 1950, and Indian and Chinese studies were added in 1952. The school was smaller than the one at London University, but larger than those at Manchester and Edinburgh, rivalling those at Oxford and Cambridge. In 1954, having outgrown its original premises in the city centre, the school moved to the Elvet Hill estate, south of the river.

The importance of oriental studies was not principally because it made Durham more attractive to students; it was because it made Durham more attractive to ambitious academics. Its purpose, the Council stated in 1951, was to act as a beacon of learning. Thacker had already negotiated the purchase of the Duke of Northumberland's Alnwick collection of Egyptian and Mesopotamian antiquities in 1949. This was possible only through the generosity of Dr H N Spalding, who, with his wife, also funded the Spalding Lecturers in Chinese and Indian Philosophy, and donated a library of 6,000 Chinese books. The Alnwick collection acted as a magnet for other donations. Over the next decade, these included the Malcolm McDonald and Loke Wan Tho collections of Chinese porcelain, part of Sir Victor Sassoon's collection of Chinese ivory and Sir Charles Hardinge's collection of Chinese jade. To house this outstanding collection of international importance, the Gulbenkian Museum of Oriental Art and Archaeology was opened at Elvet Hill in 1960, through a generous grant from the Gulbenkian Foundation.

Among the clutch of new departments formed after the war were philosophy, palaeography and diplomatic (funded by the Pilgrim Trust), archaeology (under the leadership of Eric Birley), psychology, zoology and music.

In 1946 the University completely reorganised music, following the death of Sir Edward Bairstow, the last of the non-resident Professors of Music. In the following year, the external degree was abolished and Durham became the first provincial university to establish an honours school in music. The new department's facilities were rather limited, confined to a converted divinity lecture room. But the new professor, Arthur Hutchings, was talented and energetic (if eccentric). His inaugural lecture in 1948, on humour in music, produced helpless laughter in his audience, as, part-choirboy, part-schoolmaster, part-airman, he illustrated the subject with musical interjections and sundry digressions. He was Durham's own Gerard Hoffnung. There is an apparently apocryphal story of Hutchings bumping into Miss Ethleen Scott, the Principal of St Aidan's Society. Miss Scott, finding the professor in a state of inebriation, exclaimed 'Really, Professor, drunk again!', to which Hutchings replied, 'Are you indeed, madam! So am I!' Miss Scott's successor, Dame

Students on the River Wear.

University College students at the Castle entrance, 1961.

Enid Russell-Smith, later described Hutchings, who used to address her as 'Sweet Dragon', as a genius of amiable eccentricity.

Under Hutchings, Durham's reputation for music at first outstripped many other universities. But music, like law, was low on Durham's list of priorities. Hutchings admitted that he had promised the Warden he would not complain about musical facilities until he was desperate. Remarkably, he seems to have contained himself for the best part of twelve years, until he could put up with things no longer. Staff complained that they were holding examinations in bedrooms, while Hutchings pointed out that he was in charge of the only music department in the country where every teaching room was devoid of musical instruments. 'We are on no list of priorities. We are just a nuisance. It was unkind not to say so years ago.' But he stayed. 'The Durham Music School has a reputation, spread chiefly by examiners. Either we must take advantage of that reputation or reduce.'[49]

The crisis that Hutchings alluded to was the standstill in Durham's expansion. The UGC's generosity towards Durham during the 1940s had given way to parsimony. Durham's revenue spending always outstripped grant income, while its increased scale of operations required extra expenditure that took away money earmarked for new buildings. A system was introduced where surpluses over a specified level made by any one college were redistributed among the rest, but

this was ineffective when all the colleges were losing money. Only economising enabled the division to break even during the first half of the 1950s. Capital grants were hard to come by, hence the long delays in making progress with the proposed men's college. As a result, the situation Duff had described at the end of the 1940s remained the same in the late 1950s. Attempts to hold numbers at around 1,100 failed because of the crisis in residential and teaching accommodation, and they reached nearly 1300 in 1957, making matters worse. The Warden described as 'slums' some of the properties in use on the peninsula. Two of them, 43 North Bailey, housing the history department, and Hatfield College's gatehouse, were in a state of collapse. The UGC had to be convinced, he said, that 'it is no use being beautiful unless you can also be good'.[50] Two years later the pressure on every type of accommodation was 'intolerable'.[51] The supply of lodgings in the city had dried up and there was a dearth of suitable houses. The new college, for so long planned, could not be put off any longer.

Durham's post-war development had been a reflection of the change in the British university system. As well as the foundation of the Colleges of Advanced Technology in the 1950s, plans had also been laid for several new universities, while a number of university colleges were given full university status. The University College of North Staffordshire (later Keele University) was founded in 1949, while Nottingham became a full university in 1948. Between 1952 and 1957, Southampton, Hull, Exeter and Leicester were also granted university status.

Then, in 1956, the government announced that the number of students would rise from 84,000 to 106,000 by the mid-1960s, to cater for the post-war population bulge. This second spurt of growth reinforced the primacy of residential universities over local universities. In 1957 the UGC (with Derman Christopherson, the next Warden of Durham, a member of the relevant subcommittee) decided that the expected increase in numbers was inseparable from the need for more student accommodation. In the following year it was announced that the University of Sussex would be the first of the new purpose-built universities. In parallel with this, it was necessary to devise a way of making sure that students could afford to spend three years living away from home. The Anderson Committee in 1960 proposed means-tested maintenance grants and these were enshrined in the 1962 Education Act, ensuring the viability of the new residential institutions and easing the financial path for many of the less well off.

It was also imperative to streamline the admissions system. In 1960 every applicant for a place at Durham was applying individually to each college of their choice. This was unsustainable as the volume of applications rose. By 1962 some colleges were receiving twenty-five applications

49 *Report from the Professor of Music on the state of the music school*, CDC minutes, 3 February 1959.
50 WAR, 1954–55.
51 WAR, 1956–57.

for every place. Planning a new centralised admissions system began in 1958 and the University Central Council for Admissions was fully operational in 1964.

But this expansion, although it increased the number of university students to around 120,000 by 1963, did little to alter the social composition of the expanding universities and increased only fractionally the proportion of the relevant age group attending university. So while one in eight middle-class children became university students, only one in a hundred working-class children did so. The proportion of those eligible to apply for university places rose to 4 per cent, still low by international standards; and there were hardly any more women studying at university in the early 1960s than there had been before the war.

The UGC asked Durham how many students it would wish to have by the mid-1960s. The division was understandably cautious, conscious of the pressure on the city of bringing in more students without providing the facilities for them. Durham made no increase on the number suggested ten years earlier, suggesting a target of 2000 students with 133 staff (including twenty-one professors). But while the Council's submission to the UGC reiterated existing aspirations, it also included proposals for new developments, particularly in science. Durham wanted to take advantage of yet another national campaign to improve standards of science, by increasing the number of science students and improving science facilities. The UGC was sympathetic, but there were strings attached to its approval of funding for the long-delayed new men's college and the proposed new applied science building. First, Durham should raise to 50 per cent the proportion of all students studying science; second, both the college and the science building should be built in stages and with economy in mind; and third, Durham should seek outside funding to complement the limited UGC grants. Revenue funding was expected to be applied in large part to support additional science staff and the cost of running new laboratories. Extra capital monies were promised for other major building projects so Durham could achieve its target numbers by the mid-1960s.

In June 1957 the Durham Appeal was launched as part of the division's commitment to raise external funds. At the same time, Durham also attracted a large grant from the Sir James Knott Foundation for the latest science building. The appeal, intended to raise £250,000, was closed two years later, having reached only £212,000. University fund-raising was still in its infancy. By then, work was under way on Durham's first post-war college. There was no more space on the crowded peninsula, so a site was chosen south of the river, close by the science site and not far from the new St Mary's College. The creation of the new college was closely linked with the investment in improved science facilities. The latter was the justification for admitting more students, who

Opening of Kingsgate Bridge, designed by the architect Ove Arup. The bridge was constructed in two sections, parallel to the banks, which were rotated to swing together and meet in the middle, *inset*, cutting the ribbon, *bottom*, procession across the bridge, 1963.

could only be accommodated in the planned college. Since science was still seen as a mostly male preserve, the new college would be for men. A name was agreed only in 1958. The favourite had been Cromwell, but by one vote the title of Grey College was preferred, after the reforming earl who had played an instrumental part in the University's foundation. The college admitted its first students in September 1959, although the formal opening did not take place until 1961. At the same time, work was under way on the applied science building and the reconstruction of the observatory had begun.

At the end of the 1950s, a whole series of plans was drawn up for the most ambitious expansion that the Durham colleges had ever undertaken. It was the realisation of James Duff's dream. Plans were based on the assumption of no more than 2,000 students, but after the UGC revised its estimates upwards for the 1960s and 1970s, so too did Durham. In February 1960 the Council agreed to aim for 3,000 students by the early 1970s, and only two years later for 4,500 students by the early 1980s, with the usual proviso that there should be more buildings for teaching and student accommodation.

The Council's initial ambitious scheme for the redevelop-

The Peninsula, giving a clear view of Palace Green, the Cathedral and Castle – a World Heritage Site.

Durham Castle was bequeathed to the University in 1836 by Van Mildert, the last Prince Bishop of Durham. The bishop's power was created in the 11th century by William the Conqueror who wanted a strong defence against the Scots. Chosen by the king and powerful local monks, he raised taxes, kept an army and made laws. Prince Bishops held ecclesiastical and political sovereignty over the Palatinate of Durham, the area between the rivers Tyne and Tees, plus land in Northumberland and Yorkshire. As their power and wealth grew, the Prince Bishops' fortress residence became one of the richest castles in the country. They flourished throughout the Middle Ages but their power was curtailed by Henry VIII.

ment of the area around Palace Green and North Bailey was scaled down, following discussions with the local council, alarmed at the envisaged destruction of historic buildings. Instead, plans were eventually drawn up for an extension of the library, for a new arts teaching block and a long overdue students' union building in New Elvet, and for a bridge across the river, linking Palace Green and the Bailey with New Elvet. For the science site there were proposals for a new science library and a school of engineering science. After years of pressure from the Principal, a new women's college was approved for St Aidan's. It was hoped that a 'young and untraditional architect with new ideas' could be found; in the end, Sir Basil Spence, architect of Coventry Cathedral, was commissioned. His designs, unveiled in 1961, when St Aidan's was recognised as a college, were applauded and welcomed with relief after what some described as the 'camp site' architecture of Grey College. The UGC's revised plans then led to proposals for two more men's colleges and another women's college, each for 350 students. All these colleges would be located on the once ample site now being rapidly developed south of the river. Sporting facilities were not overlooked. There were plans for a gymnasium, swimming pool and running track at Maiden Castle. The urgent need to bring together the division's growing administrative staff led to the purchase in 1962 of the former headquarters of Durham County Council. Shire Hall was an impressive Edwardian building in New Elvet that aroused strong opinions: 'The Shire Hall is held by many to be the ugliest building in Durham and no doubt it will one day be replaced by something better . . . its value is, therefore, mainly as a site'[52]. But Old Shire Hall, as it became known, never was demolished and remains the headquarters of the University.

In July 1959 the Warden announced that he would retire at the end of the following academic year. His timing was perfect. The acceleration of plans for expansion increased the impetus for Newcastle and Durham to go their separate ways. By the end of the 1950s there were some 3,500 students at Newcastle and more than 1,500 at Durham, a number that was rising steadily. On 29 January 1960 the academic board of the Newcastle Division resolved that 'the healthy development of the university now makes desirable the establishment of a University of Newcastle in place of King's College'[53]. A month later, on 23 February, the academic board of the Durham Division concurred, although many felt each side would lose a great deal in the parting. In June the Council of Durham Colleges agreed to 'acquiesce' in Newcastle's request; the Council of King's College

Derman Christopherson, Vice-Chancellor, 1960–79.

was fully supportive of the idea. The Court, invited by the Senate to consider the most effective means of achieving separation, agreed to ask for government approval of Newcastle's independence. On 21 July came agreement from the UGC and the Treasury. The decision did not just signal the creation of the University of Newcastle; it also announced the arrival of a strong and viable University of Durham. It was the culmination of everything James Duff had worked for since arriving in Durham a generation earlier. It was a great achievement.

It was left to his successor to oversee the implementation of separation. On 1 October 1960 Derman Christopherson became the last Warden of the Durham Division and the youngest university Vice-Chancellor in the country. Born in the East End of London in 1915, the son of a vicar, educated at Sherborne, Oxford and Harvard, Christopherson was a distinguished academic scientist. Awarded the OBE in 1946 for his wartime work within the Ministry of Home Security, he was elected a Fellow of Magdalene College, Cambridge, in 1945. From 1949 until 1955 he was Professor of Mechanical Engineering at Leeds University, before taking up the chair in applied science at Imperial College London. He was elected a Fellow of the Royal Society in 1960. His role as an administrator had begun with the part-time post of Bursar at Magdalene. He had been deeply involved with the governance of Imperial College and had served on various bodies linked with higher education in the UK and overseas. A tall, spare man, bespectacled, with a thick mop of hair, he spoke with a slowish, transatlantic drawl, picked up during his time as a visiting professor at the Massachusetts Institute of Technology. He described himself as moderate and tolerant, two perfect attributes for the rocky times ahead. He was keenly aware of changing student attitudes and believed that student life should be governed by as few rules as possible. 'It is up to the individual to make his own rules – that is one of the main reasons he is here.'[54]

Much had been achieved by Duff, but much remained to be done. The Durham Christopherson came to in the autumn of 1960 was still an insular place. 'Few generally well-informed people', wrote one student, 'know that Durham has a university.'[55] Of those who did, few knew it was collegiate, most believing it was red-brick. Half of all students described themselves as Anglicans, 80 per cent as Christians. Three-quarters came from middle-class backgrounds and an even higher proportion were men. Almost all of them were white.

Durham, like the rest of the country, was tentatively beginning to feel its way in interracial relations. Race was

52 WAR, 1961–62.
53 Senate minutes, 15 March 1960.
54 *Palatinate*, 26 October 1960.
55 *Palatinate*, 27 June 1961.

Facing page, The imposing entrance of Old Shire Hall on Old Elvet, built in 1896 as the headquarters of Durham County Council. It became the administrative hub of the University in 1963.

already an issue. The 1962 Commonwealth Immigrants Act for the first time restricted the rights of Commonwealth citizens to settle in the UK. It was another three years before the Race Relations Act outlawed race discrimination, and three more before Enoch Powell, the would-be classics professor, made his notorious 'River Tiber' speech. In 1962 black students in Durham were still referred to as negroes and coloureds. Relationships between whites and blacks were characterised by a certain distance, a reserve rather than hostility. Some black students were reluctant to be seen with white girls lest this should damage the reputation of the latter. Many black students felt themselves patronised by white students, who sought friendship out of a sense of duty. One reported that he found students 'only went so far in their intimacy and there was always a barrier there'.[56]

Given their backgrounds, it was unsurprising that most Durham students had moderate, conservative views – almost all of them regarded apartheid as immoral, but two-thirds were in favour of hanging only five years before it was abolished in the UK. The outside world touched Durham tangentially. Apartheid, the Congo, Algeria, the Common Market, abortion and sexuality were all among issues that concerned Durham students in the early 1960s. There were sit-down antinuclear protests on Palace Green. The world event that penetrated this comfortable haven most deeply was the Cuban missile crisis of 1962. 'The war scare on Tuesday evening', reported *Palatinate*, 'hit Durham hard. There was virtually no other topic of conversation to be heard anywhere in the University.' Many swamped the college and Union bars as an insulation from the world outside; others remained in their rooms, talking quietly, waiting for the next news bulletin. 'Lights all over Durham burned late into the night.'[57]

In relation to internal politics, a power struggle was developing between the SRC and the Union for influence over the student body. In tune with the times, the SRC was slowly becoming more assertive. The Union had shown itself too slow and too insensitive to change. Its repeated refusal to admit women until 1962, plus a string of scandals related to financial mismanagement, harmed its reputation among students. The crucial shift in influence came with approval of the plans for a students' union building, for occupation by the SRC and DCAU, that was intended to become the focus for student activities organised outside the colleges. Work on Dunelm House, as it was named, was already under way in 1962, along with Ove Arup's elegant footbridge over the Wear.

Within Durham, there was a yawning gap between the University and the city. There was very little contact between students and locals. One student hoped that 'as long as students refrain from being rude about the town's teddy boys and slum areas when they know nothing about it, we should

Durham Colleges' Rag Appeal for the Congo, 1961.

be able to live side by side, amicably making the most out of each other'.[58] The city was still marked by poverty, but for many students this meant little more than a dearth of decent eating places. Others complained that the locals lacked pride in the University. A more acerbic view was expressed by the noted north-east writer, Sid Chaplin. 'I see the students and teachers as colonists who have generally isolated themselves against the strange and somewhat unbelievable world in which they find themselves. The place has stuck in the county's crop and since it neither irritates nor pleases, it is left alone. Nobody loves it. Neither, on the other hand, is it violently hated.'[59]

Chaplin had done most of his own learning through the activities of the extramural department, one of the few parts of the University that connected with the locals. Durham claimed to be the first university to be involved in 'university extension' work. When this started in 1896, some 2,500 people attended extension lectures in literature, philosophy, history, fine art and science, but even then this type of lecture was seen as unsuitable for the local audience. It was never valued very highly by the University, which provided scarcely any finance for it. Instead, it relied on the commitment of men like Dr Jevons, through to 1928, and Dr Pace, appointed as the first, albeit part-time, director, who retired in 1947. They tutored classes for a pittance of a remuneration and with very little clerical assistance. Thanks to their efforts, the number of classes and students increased steadily, giving opportunities to men like Sid Chaplin. In 1947, H J Boyden became the first full-time director of the extramural department. He expanded the work of the department and strengthened its relationship with local authorities, so that by 1950 almost 2,000 students were attending classes.

The insularity described by Chaplin also expressed itself in the way in which student life was governed inside Durham.

56 *Palatinate*, 23 November 1962.
57 *Palatinate*, 26 October 1962.
58 *Palatinate*, 25 October 1958.
59 *Palatinate*, 7 December 1960.

Prime Minister Harold Macmillan receiving an honorary degree, 1958.

The authorities, conscious of their role as guardians of minors, were often inflexible in interpreting rules, with little regard for the way times were changing. Students, on the other hand, were usually only in favour of tinkering with the rules rather than wholesale reform. The wearing of gowns was always an issue. It was only in 1956 that they no longer had to be worn after dusk, although they were still expected for cathedral services, lectures and examinations. Yet six years later, an SRC survey found that the vast majority of students wished to continue wearing gowns to lectures. In 1956 the Principal of St Hild's introduced a crackdown on what was described as 'unseemly and embarrassing' love-making – this turned out to be couples embracing and kissing goodnight outside the college entrances. But two students wrote to *Palatinate* in support of this action. The habit had 'caused anxiety to the authorities' and lowered the dignity of the college. The newspaper remarked that if couples 'could part without passionate embraces in public, then Durham would be a nobler, finer, better-educated University'.[60] But there were also signs of simmering discontent with the stranglehold over personal freedoms exercised by most colleges. The women's training colleges were a case in point. Visiting times, for instance, particularly at weekends, were very restricted. One letter to *Palatinate*, signed by 'The Smouldering Suffragettes', noted that 'forceful guidance is given concerning entertainment and moral standards'. Control even extended to college tutors having the right to remove pictures from student rooms that did not conform to guidelines.[61]

As well as insularity, there also seemed to be an element of insecurity among Durham students.

Christopherson noticed it. 'I'm sure a lot of undergrads come here thinking they are failures. I want them to get rid of that feeling.'[62] Durham, founded in 1832, and collegiate, was sandwiched between Oxbridge and the new universities, and was uncertain of its standing. Christopherson's remarks related to the one-third of students who described themselves as Oxbridge rejects in an era when leading employers still thought Oxford and Cambridge were the only universities that mattered. Coincidentally, this proportion was almost identical with the proportion of students attracted to Durham because of the collegiate system.

The Universities of Durham and Newcastle upon Tyne Act was passed in 1963. Christopherson now became Vice-Chancellor and Warden. The Court disappeared and instead the Council became the executive body for the University, with the Senate responsible for all academic matters. The overseas colleges remained affiliated with Durham, while Sunderland Technical College, linked with the University through a quirk of history since 1905, henceforth became associated with Newcastle, where most of its students had studied. The Joint Committee on Education and Science had already gone, abolished with the consent of Durham County Council in 1959. A separate Institute of Education was re-established in Durham. As the University of Durham started a new phase in its development, the Vice-Chancellor remarked that 'we shall do everything possible to maintain in full what we think are our special advantages, and at the same time to overcome the handicaps which the small size of Durham as a University centre has in the past imposed'.[63]

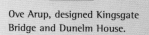

Ove Arup, designed Kingsgate Bridge and Dunelm House.

60 *Palatinate*, 18 June 1956.
61 *Palatinate*, 24 October 1958.
62 *Palatinate*, 26 October 1960.
63 WAR, 1963–64.

'In Northumberland alone both heaven and earth are seen: we walk all day on long ridges, high enough to give far views of moor and valley, and the sense of solitude above the world below . . . It is a land of far horizons, where the piled or drifted shapes of gathered vapour are for ever moving along the farthest ridge of hills, like the procession of long primeval ages that is written in tribal mounds and Roman camps and Border towers . . . '

George Trevelyan, University Chancellor, 1950–57

Stop-Go: 1963–79

DURHAM'S GROWTH WAS ALREADY WELL planned when the University went its own way. In the expectation that Durham would treble in size to 4,500 students in two decades, a huge and ambitious programme of new building was in the pipeline: three new colleges, extensions and additions to existing colleges, accommodation for graduate students, a series of new science buildings, a new arts block, the students' union, an extended library on Palace Green, a new science library, new sports facilities and even the possibility of a swimming pool and university theatre. From the UGC came a grant towards all this of £3 million for the five-year period from 1962, even though, as the Warden had pointed out, this scarcely covered the University's needs.

In 1963 higher education received fresh impetus from the Robbins Report. The report particularly wanted to widen social access to universities, and its solution was to give all those young people qualified by ability and attainment the opportunity to pursue a full-time course in higher education if they chose to do so. As at Durham, this implied an almost threefold increase in the total number of students over the next twenty years. To cater for this, Robbins wanted half a dozen new universities. Instead, existing universities were expanded, the ten Colleges of Advanced Technology (such as Aston, Brunel, Bath, Loughborough, Salford and Heriot-

St Aidan's Society, established in 1947 for women home students, was founded as a college in 1961. It became co-educational 20 years later. The College Building, designed by Basil Spence, opened in 1966.

On the Student Union terrace.

Van Mildert College, opened in 1965, is named after the last Prince Bishop of Durham, William Van Mildert, co-founder of the University in 1832.

Trevelyan College, founded in 1966, named after the historian George Macaulay Trevelyan, Chancellor of the University, 1950–57.

Watt) were given university status and the polytechnics were founded.

Although much of Durham's expansion was already planned, it was given a further stimulus. First, the UGC encouraged the University to bring forward to the early 1970s its target date for achieving 4,500 students. The University prepared a development plan, issued in 1969, based on 6,000 students. By now, however, the University was once again fretting that new teaching and other facilities were being completed more rapidly than residential accommodation. The Scarborough building for chemistry, mathematics and geology was completed in 1964. The sports hall at Maiden Castle was opened in 1965 by Clive Rowlands, captain of the Welsh rugby team, and Dunelm House in 1966, providing the centralised student facilities Durham had always lacked. The extension to the Palace Green library was completed in 1967, although, due to an oversight, the University was forced to take several feet from the roof in the following year. The New Elvet arts building was seriously delayed when the original designs were refused, but a start was made in 1965. The initial stage was finished in 1966, but nine years elapsed before it was completely finished.

Grey College's third accommodation block was completed in 1963. Then three new colleges were formally opened in successive years – St Aidan's in 1966, by Horace King, the Speaker of the House of Commons; Van Mildert in 1967, by the Archbishop of Canterbury, who, as Michael Ramsey, had been a divinity professor at Durham between 1940 and 1950; and in 1968 another women's college, Trevelyan, named after the great historian, G M Trevelyan,

Facing page, Dunelm House, home of Durham Students' Union since the 1960s.

Collingwood College, founded in 1972 as Durham's first purpose-built mixed college.

Chancellor of the University from 1933 to 1958, by Lord Butler, the architect of the 1944 Education Act. At the same time, Durham pioneered the provision of accommodation for married graduates. The twenty-nine unfurnished flats built at Kepier Court in 1966 were the first to be provided by any UK university. The University also shook off the last vestiges of dogmatic Anglicanism when Ushaw College, a Roman Catholic seminary established in Durham in 1808, was licensed as a hall of residence by the University in 1968.

The problem was that in those five years Durham's student population had risen from less than 2,000 to almost 3,000, of whom almost 1,000 were women. The rate of growth in numbers since 1961 had been more than 11 per cent every year. The city was full of students struggling to find somewhere to live. Every letting room was taken. In 1965 Parsons Field House was built as a transit camp for students waiting to join the new colleges. Even the delayed completion in 1973 of the latest new college, named after Sir Edward Collingwood, a former chairman of Council – did little to alter the pressure on space. In protest, a group of student squatters briefly occupied a house in the Gilesgate area of the city. By then, the financial situation had changed for the worse and the University had to look beyond state grants to fund more residential places.

Since 1945, every time the state had sanctioned an expansionary phase in the development of British universities, it had been justified as part of an intermittent crusade to promote science. The forecasts based on Robbins were no different and, as in the past, never lived up to expectations. Durham had been encouraged to attract more science students in the late 1940s and the late 1950s. After Robbins, Durham was urged to achieve parity between the number of arts and science students. Yet the University would fail to attract enough science students for the places it had available. Nevertheless, the development of the sciences was a necessary part of the University's curriculum plans. Separation from Newcastle, for so long the purveyor of most science teaching, was one stimulus. Bill Musgrave, Lecturer in Chemistry since 1945, was appointed to the second chair in chemistry in 1960, and proved to be hugely influential in the department's development. Engineering science was established in 1964 under Professor Russell Hoyle. In the following year, Gordon Higgins became the first Professor of Civil Engineering, while Martin Bott was appointed to a personal chair in geophysics in 1966. The outstanding reputation of the University in

Students at work, left to right,1960s, 70s and 80s.

geology was sustained, after the departure of Kingsley Dunham in 1967, by the appointment of the second successive Durham graduate to head the department. This was Malcolm Brown, who had graduated from Durham with first class honours in geology in 1950. He followed Wager to Oxford, where he remained, barring excursions as a visiting fellow to the USA, until he came to Durham. His studies in petrology gained him an international reputation that worked to Durham's advantage. He left, as had his predecessor, to lead the Institute of Geological Sciences in 1979, four years after his election as a Fellow of the Royal Society, and he was knighted in 1985. Another influential academic in the University was Bill Fisher, Professor of Geography since 1956. A brilliant lecturer and prolific author, he had an immense impact. He developed a broadly based and productive department and was regarded with respect and affection by many of those he taught. With a strong interest in Middle East studies, he became the first director of the new Centre for Middle Eastern and Islamic Studies, formed to coordinate cross-curricular interest in the subject. This in turn spawned the department of anthropology in 1967.

Robbins also looked at teacher training, and this too had implications for Durham. In 1965 the degree of Bachelor of Education was introduced for students at teacher training colleges. In Durham, where Bede, St Hild's and Neville's Cross expanded rapidly, the University was happy to leave admissions to the colleges, but insisted that entry requirements should be the same for the BEd as for the BA and BSc. Two years after the BEd, the Postgraduate Certificate of Education (PGCE) was introduced, which saw a rise in postgraduate students coming to Durham. Combined with a lack of college accommodation at the time, this influx led to the formation of the Graduate Society in 1965, under the direction of Professor Fisher. In the 1960s, the University developed plans to expand the curriculum that were as ambitious as its building programme. Some fell by the wayside, including proposals to establish fine art, drama and architecture and an Institute of European Studies. Russian and Italian were introduced, and in 1964 second-year language students were sent to study abroad for the first time. One of the greatest curricular expansions during the 1960s came from the renewed development of social sciences. While the expected increase in applications for science did not materialise, there was a huge interest in social sciences. In 1963–64 the department of social studies was divided into the departments of politics, economics, law, and social theory and institutions. From two lecturers when the department was formed in 1946, there were now thirty-five members of staff in four disciplines. An important part of the department was the Business School, formed in consultation with local industrialists as a centre for industrial research in 1960. Initially known as the business research

unit, it was made permanent in 1965, the same year the business schools in London and Manchester were formed. The departments of economic history and anthropology were also formed in 1965. New honours courses were introduced in social theory and administration, economics, economics and psychology, economics and economic history, law, anthropology, and anthropology with either psychology or sociology. The BA in social studies had served its purpose and was abolished in 1969. A separate faculty of social sciences was created in 1967–68, followed by a faculty of law in 1970. As well as the rising number of joint honours courses, the general arts and science degrees were also revised to offer greater scope and continuity.

The notion that general degrees were a passport to university for those whose sporting or acting abilities outshone their intellectual attainments was voiced openly by the University's founding Professor of Social Theory and Institutions. John Rex came to Durham from the sociology chair at the University of Birmingham in 1964. A political exile from the apartheid regime in South Africa, he arrived in the UK in 1949. His success in creating an outstanding department in Durham led him to repeat the exercise with the University of Warwick, which he joined in 1970. His eminence was recognised while he was at Durham when he was appointed as a member of the UNESCO International Experts' Committee on Racism and Race Prejudice in 1967. Widely published, he went on to hold posts at several other universities at home and overseas. His successor, Philip Abrams, reinforced Rex's achievement, confirming the department's leading reputation.

Rex's opinions ruffled feathers in conservative Durham. The Principal of one college even described Rex as a far leftist. Rex was a supporter of causes such as the Campaign for Nuclear Disarmament, but his passion was the defeat of apartheid in southern Africa and he never believed the British really understood what drove African nationalism. He was certainly charismatic. One of his first honours students was Richard Adams, later founder of Tearcraft and Traidcraft. He recalled that Rex told them that he would have failed if they became social workers. 'Your job is to change society!'[64] At an open SRC meeting to discuss the nature of the University in 1968, Rex stated: 'I have sometimes been asked to look at application forms I have rejected because of the school [the student] attended, the home he came from, whether he has a sporting record, or because of what his father is'.[65] His allegations were promptly dismissed by heads of colleges and the University Registrar.

Rex's questioning of the purpose of the University in an open student forum was a sign of the rebellious times. The Vice-Chancellor was overseeing not just the biggest and most rapid expansion of the University in its history, but also a fundamental change in student opinion. There were rum-

64 *Durham First*, Spring 2001.
65 *Palatinate*, 24 October 1968.

Michael Heseltine, Conservative politician at his daughter's graduation, 1993.

girl. 'It was partly for this kind of person that the Medical Centre was created and it would surely have been more humane to have attempted positive corrective measures than to have dismissed the girl out of hand.'[68] St Aidan's JCR regretted that the authorities were taking moral considerations into account, believing that the sexual morality of students was their own affair. Their Principal, on the other hand, the redoubtable Dame Enid Russell-Smith, strongly disapproved of sex outside marriage, and even more so of illegitimate children (the first in Durham was born to a St Aidan's student in 1964).

A University medical officer (UMO) had been appointed only in 1964, with the Student Medical Centre opening only in 1965, even though there had been repeated pleas from students for such a service since the late 1940s. In the early 1960s the UMO adopted a paternal approach to sex. Three women students writing on contraception in March 1965 believed that more women were losing their virginity at university and should therefore seek as much advice about sex and contraception as possible. But they found that for a single woman this was easier said than done, especially in the north. The Family Planning Association officially helped only married women and engaged couples. The names of enlightened doctors might be obtained from local pharma-

Launch of a student journal, *Phalanx,* 1968.

blings in Durham throughout the early 1960s, but there always seemed to be a tension between the instinctive conservatism of most Durham students and their aspiration to be given greater responsibility for their own lives. One St Aidan's student from the early 1960s, Rowena Collins, recalled plenty of drinking and 'a good deal of illicit sex', but could not remember anyone taking drugs.[66] Ten years later, in 1971, a student survey discovered 'an absence of free love, a distinct lack of pot smokers, and the presence only of a few people willing to become actively politically involved'.[67]

One celebrated incident indicative of the times was the Cummin-Dawson case in 1964. Gillian Dawson from St Aidan's was discovered to have spent the night with Deryck Cummin, a St Cuthbert's student. Both students were eventually rusticated, despite previously exemplary records. What was interesting was not the predictable response of the college authorities, but the diverse reaction of St Aidan's JCR on the one hand and *Palatinate* on the other. Both agreed the measures taken were out of proportion, but *Palatinate* defended the strict regulations governing the women's colleges on the grounds that most women students coming up to Durham were from sheltered backgrounds. The newspaper favoured referring Dawson to the Medical Centre. She was, remarked the paper, a sensitive

66 Quoted in Rodmell, *G E St Aidan's – from Home Students to Society to College,* Durham, 1997, p.70.
67 *Palatinate,* 18 November 1971.

68 *Palatinate,* 9 December 1964.

Under Elvet Bridge. The River Wear comes alive with boats of all shapes and sizes, from fine sculling boats to sixty foot long eights to pleasure boats.

cists if persistent requests were made. The policy of the University was to provide female contraceptives only for medical and psychiatric reasons. 'It is impossible to obtain contraceptives for women in the Durham area by "legitimate" means'.[69] The UMO, Dr Munro, responded that those in such a situation were in a minority and that the University had to take into account students, their parents and families, and local and national public opinion. He suggested that a request for contraceptive advice was 'a symptom of a more basic need for youthful guidance . . . it is not a contraceptive that is required but a husband, or a flat, or a new course of study'.[70]

This approach would have to change. In 1967 the NHS (Family Planning) Act allowed health authorities to give contraceptive advice to anyone, regardless of marital status. In the same year, both abortion and homosexuality were legalised. A more understanding view was adopted at the Student Medical Centre, although this tended to lag behind student opinion. Freshers were finally issued with a frank handbook on birth control for the first time in 1974, when there were still complaints that the University doctors were too often 'starchy and too ready to preach morals'. In the same year, Yeast, the gay students' society, was founded, one student writing that for too long 'homosexuality and bisexuality have been locked away like skeletons rattling in a cupboard along with sex before marriage and feminism'.[71] Only three years previously, the UMO had declared that it was impossible for any student to be categorised as homosexual since 'they hadn't yet had a chance to discover their own sexuality, let alone resolve it'.[72]

A national debate was already taking place in 1967 on lowering the age of majority from twenty-one to eighteen. The Family Law Reform Act was passed in 1969 and from 1 January 1970 undergraduates were regarded as adults. Over this period, the University, particularly college heads, were inching their way towards change. The new colleges, Van Mildert, Trevelyan and, later, Collingwood, without any historical baggage, were leading the way. Durham during the late 1960s was in the vanguard of British universities in developing mixed colleges, governed in a more informal way appropriate to the times. In 1967, for instance, Van Mildert pressed for the freedom to co-opt students as members of the college governing body. St Mary's was the only other college interested. Two years later the senior men and women emphasised the importance of such links between student bodies and the college governing bodies, telling Council that they could only strengthen the collegiate system.

Van Mildert pioneered mixing men and women in the same college. During its first years, when the college had spare rooms, they were let to women students from other colleges to alleviate the crisis in overcrowding. It had been a

positive experience and, given other changes, encouraged the college to pursue the idea with the University. It was said that most college heads – and probably most students outside the new colleges – were happy with the status quo, but had open minds about mixed colleges. The opposition to Van Mildert's plans was described by a future Principal of the college as 'much of it irrational and some frankly dishonest'.[73] Consent was given by the Senate in February 1971, with a maximum female quota of 20 per cent. This was ignored by the college and outlawed under the Sex Discrimination Act of 1975.

At the time, the Senate agreed to the principle of colleges going mixed provided this had the support of three-quarters of both the governing body and student body concerned. The last of the new colleges, Collingwood, had been considered as a mixed college when plans were first suggested in 1963. This was an advanced concept for the time, so much so that although nine years would elapse before the college opened, Collingwood was still the first student accommodation in the country to mix rooms on the same landings and in the same blocks. In May 1971, the Senate agreed that Collingwood students should be split equally between men and women. The Registrar, Ian Graham, was hostile to the idea, insisting that the overall ratio within the University, of 3:1 in favour of men, should be retained. His resistance was prolonged and inflexible, but ultimately in vain. By the time Collingwood was opened in 1972, the college broke with Durham's traditional past in almost every respect. Collingwood's men and women, happily living next door to each other, were free to come and go as they pleased and welcome visitors at any time of the day or night, although consent was needed for overnight visits. The acceptance of students as adults breathed fresh air through the corridors of the older colleges as well. In St Mary's, for instance, students were given individual room keys, keys for the front door, the right to live out and greater freedom to have visitors. The college system had proved adaptable to change.

All this was taking place during the waxing and waning of student protest across the world. British universities escaped most of the violence. One St Aidan's student, Ingrid Burmeister, spending her year out studying French in Paris in 1968, recalled that she and her friends had been terrified by the violence and were relieved to return to the calm of Durham. Although the London School of Economics was closed for three weeks during 1969, and almost every university between 1968 and 1973 experienced sit-ins of varying duration, protest was less hectic, less protracted, less violent, less overtly political and more parochial in the UK in general.

British students may have been less passionate in their politics, but even in moderate, conservative Durham, the 1960s and early 1970s represented an era of regular politi-

69 *Palatinate*, 10 March 1966.
70 *Palatinate*, 28 April 1966.
71 *Palatinate*, 24 October 1974.

72 *Palatinate*, 4 November 1971
73 Bradshaw, A., Van Mildert College – *The First 25 Years: A Sketch*, Durham, 1990, p.11.

cal protest. Opposition to apartheid in South Africa was constructive as well as demonstrative. With the support of the SRC and the Vice-Chancellor, St Cuthbert's organised a scholarship appeal that raised funds to bring a South African student to study in Durham. The first was Marcus Balintulo, who attended Hatfield in 1965 to study social theory and institutions under Professor Rex. A later scholarship-holder was not so lucky, having his passport withdrawn to stop him leaving the country. Vietnam was also topical, although in Durham it was more written about than anything else. There were campaigns to persuade businesses to pull out of Pinochet's Chile as well as apartheid-era South Africa, against the anti-union legislation of the Ted Heath government, and in sympathy with the victims of the disfiguring drug thalidomide.

Many of these campaigns were organised by the SRC, or, as it became briefly, the Durham Colleges' Students Association, and then finally, in 1970, the Durham Students' Union (DSU). Three things had shot the SRC to a position of greater influence. The first was separation from Newcastle, which resulted in funding that had previously been split between two divisions being allocated entirely to Durham's SRC. The second was the building of Dunelm House and its potential to raise funds for the SRC. The third was the

Student demonstration, 1971.

Mo Mowlam, Labour politician, on a visit to Durham in 1988. She was active in student politics and graduated in Anthropology in 1971.

decline of the Union Society. But DSU lacked strength in a collegiate university. The college junior common rooms (JCRs) were an effective counterweight. Unless all were in harmony, DSU's influence was neutered. There were accusations of apathy from the more politically committed, but it was less apathy than moderation and disinterest in student affairs. But the debates on the floor of Dunelm House were a training ground for several budding politicians, notably Mo Mowlam, a future Labour cabinet minister, and Edward Leigh, a future Conservative minister.

The main issue at stake during the protests was student involvement in university governance. There was as much anxiety among the authorities in Durham as elsewhere about the wisdom of appointing students as members of university decision-making bodies. Two Durham academics signed a letter with 150 others in 1970, condemning student violence and disputing the right of students to vote on committees concerned with academic matters. But Derman Christopherson recognised the tardiness of university authorities to accept the changed role of young people in society. As chairman of the CVCP from 1967, he was at the heart of the negotiations with the National Union of Students that reached a settlement on this issue. In Durham, by 1967, there was already a joint committee of Council and the SRC, which discussed changes to the way student life

Graduation smiles.

Boat Club 1st VIII with their trophies, 1971–72, coached by Eric Halladay, far left.

was regulated. There was agreement that students should have a greater say in issues affecting student welfare, more limited influence in academic matters and none in relation to admissions and appointments. Rules governing student discipline were also overhauled. There were several departmental joint forums and the colleges improved the way they consulted with students. Then, in 1969, the SRC president was invited to join Council. Christopherson, who was surely well placed to judge, paid tribute to the moderate and realistic approach of student officers and representatives in Durham. His service to British universities was recognised with a knighthood in 1969.

The relative calm of Durham in a turbulent sea of educational unrest came under parliamentary scrutiny in 1969, when the Select Committee on Science and Education looked at student relations. Durham was the only collegiate university visited by committee members, but it was clear from their report that they believed the collegiate system had a lot to do with the harmonious coexistence of students and staff. The colleges, suggested the committee, were an effective safety valve for stress. Their small size within a growing university contributed to stable relationships, while expansion brought younger staff, with a more sympathetic approach towards students, into the colleges and departments. This conclusion

Eric Halladay, historian, Master of Grey College, 1980–89 and coach to Durham University crews for 32 years. He helped Durham to become one of the premier rowing universities in the UK. He was a key adviser in the planning of the Northumbrian Water University Boat Race, and one of his final services to rowing was as an official at the inaugural race in 1997.

was a suitable riposte for some in the University who believed that centralised admissions, expanding departments and a stronger SRC were diluting the college ethos.

The committee also commented on Durham's low failure rate (half the national average), which it attributed to the partnership between colleges and departments in the assessment and admission of students, the calibre of applicants and the ability of students to switch subjects at the end of their first year. In the late 1960s, approximately 40 per cent of all students were graduating from Durham with first or upper second class degrees.

There were some in Durham who believed that the admissions system was less than perfect. University education was still very much a minority experience in the UK, and the lack of breadth in Durham's student population caused unease. The general arts degree (the general science degree was abolished in 1965) was considered by some as a backdoor route into Durham for the brilliant sportsperson with lesser academic attainments. The system was defended vigorously by Dr Whitworth, the often intemperate Master of Hatfield College. While he admitted that 37 per cent of his own college intake came from independent schools, he stressed that nearly 60 per cent came from state schools and 80 per cent from modest income backgrounds. He admitted that the general degree did require lower entry qualifications and that many of those taking up places were indeed excellent sportspeople, but he also pointed out that most candidates for honours degrees came with three B grades at A level, which beat Oxbridge hands down at the time.

It would have been physically impossible for general degree students to have been solely responsible for the higher sporting standards obvious from the pages of *Palatinate* during this period. Durham was expanding, had a larger pool of talent to choose from and better facilities for them to use. Maiden Castle soon proved inadequate for the greater numbers of students taking part in sport, but more playing fields were developed, linked by a bridge over the river, and an all-weather pitch was laid during the early 1970s. By 1972, there were forty-one sports clubs, with an aggregate of 4,400 student members, while sixteen colleges were involved in various intercollegiate trophies. Rowing was the most popular team sport, squash and tennis the most popular individual sports. Under Eric Halladay, history don, Vice-Master of Grey College and outstanding amateur rowing coach, the DUBC 1st VIII repeatedly won the UAU championship, achieving ten wins in a row between 1966 and 1975. The University squash team won its first UAU title in 1968 and retained the championship the following year.

The two other major team sports, rugby and cricket, reached new heights. With Hartley Elliott as coach, the University rugby team shared the UAU title in 1965 and then beat deadly rivals Newcastle to win the championship in 1969. 'The calibre of players then in the university was exceptional and this was very much a function of Elliott's recruitment of his players, his enthusiasm and his ability to arrange a quality fixture list.'[74] Among these players was Grey student Peter Dixon, later captain of England. After Elliott retired, Ted Wood took up his mantle in 1974, when he came to Durham as Academic Bursar at Hatfield. Rugby at Durham continued to flourish in his care. A well-respected rugby player, he was an even more outstanding coach, whose advice was sought frequently at national level. The University's cricketers won the UAU title in 1972 for the first time since the days of Frank Tyson, repeating the feat two years later. On the latter occasion the leading batsman was Bede student Gehan Mendis, later of Sussex, while the two outstanding players from this generation were batsman Graeme Fowler and bowler Paul Allott, who both later played for England.

Among other sporting achievements, Pete Holt of Grey became Durham's first triple UAU champion, winning his third cycling title in 1965. This was the time when Brian Clough was briefly coaching the University soccer team. At various times in the 1960s and 1970s there were title successes for Durham's athletics, fencing, swimming and

74 *Palatinate*, 20 June 1997.

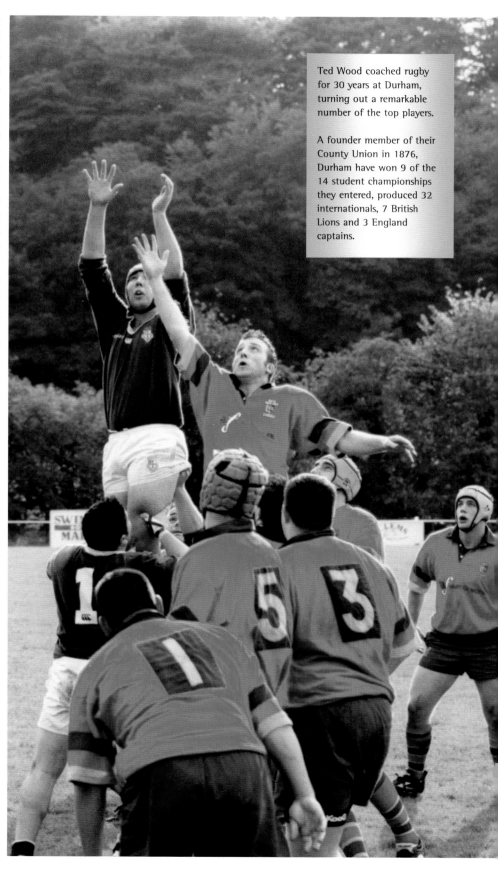

Ted Wood coached rugby for 30 years at Durham, turning out a remarkable number of the top players.

A founder member of their County Union in 1876, Durham have won 9 of the 14 student championships they entered, produced 32 internationals, 7 British Lions and 3 England captains.

women's lacrosse teams.

To judge from the pages of *Palatinate*, live music was one of the most vibrant aspects of student life in the late 1960s and early 1970s. Student bands began to appear for the first time, groups such as The String of Bedes and the Greyhounds. The high point was probably 1967. During Rag Week in February, classical fans could hear the great Russian pianist Shura Cherkassky, or the outstanding British organist Gillian Weir, while the featured artists at the Rag Ball included Alan Price, Chris Farlowe and Chuck Berry. Dunelm House, where jazz pianist Thelonius Monk had played at the opening in 1966, hosted some of the top names in UK popular music. The event everybody talked about in February 1967 was the appearance of Eric Burdon and The Animals. The concert was expected to make a loss, profits from previous events being ploughed in to support it. But demand was so high that SRC cards were forged and burly merchant seamen impersonated students. Peter Axten, one of the organisers, recalled that after word got out, the publicity produced 'busloads from the depths of Northumberland and elsewhere. We were petrified about having to turn people away . . . so we just kept letting them in'.[75] With 1,600 people crowding in to hear the band, the result was a bumper profit. Perhaps some of this was reinvested in bringing Pink Floyd to Durham in October the same year. One student, Pamela Meadows, has never forgotten the occasion; it was a spectacle that had to be seen as well as heard – 'it was a truly mind-blowing experience'.[76] The top act at the June Ball in 1968 (when double tickets cost four guineas) was The Who, while The Hollies played in 1969. The last great year for live popular music was 1971, when the list of acts appearing in Durham included Mungo Jerry, Rick Wakeman's Strawbs, Humble Pie, Uriah Heep, Wishbone Ash and Supertramp. But by the following year, fewer students were turning up to these events and they petered out.

In 1974 the city's first nightclub, Klute, opened its doors, quickly becoming a student haunt. Pub crawls were still a staple of student life – in 1965 *Palatinate* listed forty-three drinking establishments in and around Durham. There were always problems because too much was drunk. In December 1965, when a drunken riotous group of students from St Cuthbert's led an assault on St Aidan's, all college Christmas dinners were banned the following year. Dame Enid Russell-Smith complained, 'I don't think a twentieth-century university can tolerate eighteenth-century standards of conduct'.[77] June Week vanished without any mourning in 1968, although the June Ball was retained. Rag Week was

A psychedelic John Lennon, of the Beatles, made the front cover of rag magazine, *Purple Patch*, 1969.

moved around the calendar and renamed DUCK (Durham University Charities Kommittee) Week in 1977. There was still no university theatre, but the standard of drama in Durham rose nevertheless, as student actors began to appear for the first time in the finals of the NUS Drama Festival and carried on taking plays to the Edinburgh Festival Fringe, as they had since the mid-1950s.

The University has never had a theatre of its own. The theatre, like the swimming pool, was a victim of a more parsimonious approach to university funding. The ink on the Robbins Report barely had time to dry before the financial brakes were applied by government because of the worsening state of the economy. The UGC cut back its capital commitments and looked for cheaper options. In Durham, despite the protests of the Vice-Chancellor, as well as the Treasurer, Colonel Fitzgerald-Lombard, projects like the theatre and the pool never reached the drawing board, while others that were already there gathered dust. So a start on Collingwood, which should have gone ahead in 1964, was delayed until 1969, when less expensive plans had been drawn up and the University had sold property in Middlesex to meet half the costs. The new life sciences building was also delayed for several years, while the arts building in New Elvet had to be built in stages and was not completed until 1974. Plans for a new central library were constantly deferred, even after approval had been given, and it was not built until the early 1980s. Instead, in 1977, the library took over the premises occupied by the Union Society, which moved over the green to the Pemberton Building. With capital grants severely cut back, one new student block, Moatside, for University College, was financed through commercial loans, but the standards of the completed building, with its tiny rooms, left a lot to be desired. Instead, the colleges set aside income from vacation lettings to finance new buildings and took out loans serviced by the larger income accruing from greater student numbers.

As early as 1966 members of staff had expressed their 'grave disquiet at the evidence of the continuance of stop-go financing of university expansion, and the present atmosphere of uncertainty concerning the finance'.[78] In the following year, as the money available for the next quinquennium was reduced, Durham's colleges had to accept limits on the number of students for each department. In the late 1960s, the government believed things were so bad that it was considering a whole host of measures to cut costs, including student loans instead of grants, career restrictions on grant-aided students, increased fees for over-

75 *Durham First*, Autumn 1998.
76 *Durham First*, Autumn 1998.
77 Quoted in Rodmell, p.119.
78 Senate minutes, 17 May 1966.

A dinner jacketed unicylist and an atheletic juggler raising money for charity, 1990. In 2006, the University's charity committee DUCK raised nearly a quarter of a million pounds.

seas students, fast-stream shorter degrees, the sharing of facilities between institutions, and higher staff-student ratios. It was a sign of things to come. The Vice-Chancellor was concerned that politicians had a false impression that university education was capital-intensive, when really the spending of the last decade had been to catch up on long-deferred projects and to prepare for the increased number of students. He was also worried that financial considerations were obscuring the real value of universities. 'A university,' he wrote, 'is not an organisation whose success or failure can be measured in financial terms.'[79]

Castle drainpipe

Many of the measures contemplated by the government occurred by default as rising costs and inflation imposed self-restraint on the universities. Then, during the oil crisis of the early 1970s, the government took emergency action, announcing that grants would no longer take inflation into account. Notice of this change came only after the universities had made offers to students. In Durham the result was cost-cutting in areas that did not affect the life of the University, coupled with a freeze on vacancies and the postponement of new posts. Fears for the future of the colleges were expressed, and the relationship between colleges, departments and the University administration became strained as financial priorities had to be set.

All this was happening at the same time as teacher training was being reformed yet again. This time contraction was on the cards, given a declining school population. But there was also a renewed push towards an all-graduate profession. The James Report, at the end of 1971, was the catalyst for wholesale change. Some teacher training colleges closed, others were merged, most were transformed. By the late 1970s, almost half of all teacher training places had been axed. In Durham the Institute of Education and Department of Education were

merged to create the School of Education, responsible for PGCE and BEd students and research work. Neville's Cross was amalgamated with Durham Technical College to form New College outside the University. The colleges of St Hild's and Bede had combined two years earlier in anticipation of moving towards integration within the University as an all-undergraduate college. With fewer teaching places, other departments, particularly in science, absorbed many of the new undergraduates. Durham was actually teaching more students while its budget was going down.

Rampant inflation forced the abandonment of the quinquennial funding system. It was no longer possible to estimate with any certainty either what funding the universities would need or whether the government would be able to provide it. Financial planning became almost impossible for the universities, which, Christopherson noted in 1978, were now 'living from hand to mouth'.[80] At Durham in 1975, for instance, only half of all vacant posts were being filled, the maintenance and building budget was slashed, library opening hours and book funds were cut, light switches in colleges were taped over and bedders were placed on a three-day week. With a decline in spending per student of 60 per cent in real terms between 1969 and 1979, Durham, in preserving undergraduate teaching, had 'done great harm to both taught postgraduate courses and to research work'.[81] As Margaret Thatcher's government came to power in 1979, with the intention of pruning back state involvement and state expenditure, this situation was unlikely to change. Sir Derman Christopherson had announced his retirement in the previous year, returning to Cambridge, where he was Master of Magdalene College until 1985. Until his successor arrived, Professor Musgrave acted as Vice-Chancellor.

The colleges of St Hild and St Bede were separate foundations of the mid-19th century. They were amalgamated in 1975 to become the College of St Hild and St Bede which then became fully incorporated into the university.

79 WAR, 1970–71.
80 WAR, 1977–78.
81 WAR, 1978–79.

Facing page, The Castle, Palace Green and Framwellgate Bridge.

Success under Stress: 1980–92

WHEN PROFESSOR FRED HOLLIDAY ARRIVED in Durham in January 1980, as the new Vice-Chancellor, he was invited to dinner at Hatfield. The beef joint brought into the hall had not been carved. At the top table Dr Peter Reynolds, chairman of Council, offered Holliday the carving knife – he wanted to see how good he was at resource allocation. For Holliday, this was a typical example of Durham's relaxed atmosphere, but Reynolds was also making a serious point. There were challenging times ahead for the University and its new Vice-Chancellor.

Holliday was in his early forties, quite young for a Vice-Chancellor. A graduate of Sheffield University, he came to Durham from Aberdeen, where he had been Professor of Zoology. Previously he had acted as Principal of Stirling University. He was a great believer in taking higher education into the wider world. He served on numerous public bodies and was chairman of the Nature Conservancy Council. When he visited Durham it was a frosty night, and he was spellbound by Palace Green, where the elms were touched by hoar frost and the cathedral seemed to be floating among them. It was a magical vision and the new Vice-Chancellor never lost the feeling that Durham was his Camelot. He found people in Durham warm and welcoming, and within the University there was energy and purpose, 'albeit frustrated in many

Clockwise from top left, Demonstration against cuts in university funding outside Old Shire Hall, 1986. Students protesting against apartheid in South Africa, 1986. Durham Says Yes to Fair Access, demonstration in London, 2006.

respects by financial stringency.[82] Holliday spent one month in each of five colleges to get a feel for a collegiate university, of which he had no previous experience. Businesslike, efficient and approachable, with a managerial instinct, Holliday seemed well suited to the task of steering the University through the stormy waters ahead. 'Call me Fred!' he said – but very few dared.

There were already clear signs of the course being charted for the universities by Margaret Thatcher's government. Under Mark Carlisle and Sir Keith Joseph, Secretaries of State for Education and Science between 1979 and 1986, university spending was expected to remain with cash limits. The UGC's initial tack was to encourage universities to cut back on their annual intake to preserve the quality of teaching and research. But at the end of 1980 the government sharply reduced the money available for the foreseeable future. By the end of 1984 the budgets of Britain's universities were 13 per cent less in real terms. The UGC did not share these reductions equally among all universities. It became difficult to predict where cuts were going to be made next. In general, the UGC tried to maintain courses in science, technology and business studies that were in line with government thinking.

Driving down costs was all part of the government's policy of embedding the virtues of economy and efficiency

within a system it regarded as both spendthrift and failing to produce graduates as wealth-makers. Universities became even more circumscribed in their ability to set their own priorities when the system of block grants was replaced by the creation of what were known as units of resource, where funds were tied directly to students and used to compare the cost-effectiveness of each university. This was a much more vivid demonstration of what Derman Christopherson had expressed alarm about a decade earlier. The trend towards efficiency based on a business model was confirmed by the Jarratt Report in 1985, which envisaged Vice-Chancellors as chief executives, set free from the traditional cumbersome university decision-making machinery. In Fred Holliday, Durham University already had an embryonic chief executive.

Holliday came to a university where, even before the cutbacks of the 1980s, little money had been spent on infrastructure for some years. The University was already striving to raise as much income as possible from research grants and vacation lettings in the colleges in order to maintain standards. At least approval for a start to be made on the new central library came before further savings were demanded in the summer of 1981. Durham lost 300 students, 70 staff and £1 million a year. For Holliday, the 'savage cuts'.[83] imposed on the universities merited the res-

82 WAR, 1979.
83 *Palatinate*, 28 January 1982.

ignation of the UGC. The initial response of the Vice-Chancellor and the University's new Treasurer, Alec McWilliam, was to protect academic departments as far as possible by pruning costs from non-academic activities.

This policy made the relationship between the University and the colleges more difficult. Fred Holliday appreciated that it was the colleges which made Durham different. The phrase, 'Durham is different',[84] has been attributed to the University Registrar at the time, Ian Graham. He first came to Durham in 1950 as Assistant Registrar, taking over as Registrar on separation from Newcastle in 1963. He was killed in a car crash on Boxing Day 1984. Completely committed to the University, with a keen interest in rugby and drama, Graham's service, wrote the Vice-Chancellor, 'to the student body through knowledge, advice, goodwill and friendship was undoubtedly his greatest gift'.[85] He was succeeded by John Hayward.

Holliday also appreciated that the colleges had been neglected (like other parts of the University) during the 1970s and were badly in need of reinvestment. The University had pursued a deliberate policy of keeping increases in maintenance fees, charged on behalf of the colleges, below the rate of inflation. This was because the value of student grants was also being eroded and the University did not wish to deter prospective students from coming to Durham, nor place any undue financial pressure on existing students. But the cumulative effect was increasing wear and tear in the colleges. They had been trying to make up the difference in other ways, mainly through income raised from vacation conferences.

The colleges felt they were being required to shoulder more and more financial responsibilities, while being denied a realistic maintenance fee that still provided them with most of their income. This was not a view universally accepted. There were regular protests from students that maintenance fees were too high. In the departments there was also a body of opinion that the colleges were a costly burden the University could no longer afford. However, as an article in *Palatinate* later pointed out, it was the college system that drew students to Durham in the first place. They identified strongly with their colleges, which, in return, provided them with a system of support that produced the lowest university dropout rate in the country. During the 1980s, many of Durham's colleges also went mixed. Some saw this as making Durham's collegiate system more attractive to prospective students; others believed it diminished the individuality of the colleges. St Aidan's went mixed in 1981, Grey in 1985, University College in 1987 and, in controversial decisions driven by governing bodies in the face of student opposition, Hatfield in 1988 and, finally, Trevelyan in 1992.

Some traditions remained intact, such as the college bedders. 'Bedders are notorious for plunging into rooms with no apparent warning. Actually, they always knock, but it is debatable whether this comes before or after the door has swung open to expose a horrified couple to an appreciative audience in the corridors. (Sometimes it isn't a couple.)'[86] Some were regarded almost as surrogate mothers – one in University College was once sent a large box of chocolates on Mother's Day, with a card that read 'To our second Mum'.

In 1983 Durham was asked to find savings of another 2 per cent per student. The Vice-Chancellor was certain this would destroy Durham. Even cuts of half as much would seriously damage teaching and research. Two years later the government announced a fundamental change in the way

Princess Anne on a visit to Durham University with Vice-Chancellor Fred Holliday, 1988.

84 Rodmell, p. 171.
85 *Palatinate*, 31 January 1985.
86 *Palatinate*, 11 May 1989.

Students throw themselves into fundraising for DUCK, 1984–88. *Above, clockwise from top left,* Tim Harrison, Matthew Kingdom, Guy Reed and Paul Windsor lived on a raft, 1984; sponsored cycle round the UK, 1988; Becky Frank and Andrew Reine, 1987; Charity hairdo – Marcus Stevens raised £250; 'Back to School', 1986; *Below,* 1986; Kilimanjaro, Save the Children 2005; Jailbreak; Thousands of ducks start their annual DUCK race, 2006.

Oriental Museum keeper, John Ruffle and Gloria Juniper, 1986.

that the utility of education should be based on the profession trade of the pupil.' He believed that Durham's purpose should be to influence the ideas, aspirations and cultures through which every individual related to another. These ideals 'lead to objectivity, fairmindedness, honesty, reliability, understanding, compassion, altruism and wisdom'. He emphasised that Durham would do everything to prevent a narrowing of the curriculum it offered. 'We are a distinctive University, offering a balance of fundamental subjects, and we wish to remain so. We have blended advanced technology with the humanities successfully.'[87] A year later he succinctly summarised the University's objectives: the highest standards in teaching and research; the retention of a broad range of courses; the strengthening of cultural and commercial ties locally; and the widening of access to mature students and those within the state sector, without any diminution of quality. It would have made for an easy life to accept the cuts, but Holliday had different ideas.

The University strove to maintain a balanced range of courses during the budget cuts of the 1980s. Hard choices had to be made and some courses disappeared, some long-standing independent departments were merged with others, some staff took early retirement and some vacancies,

Fred Holliday, Vice-Chancellor, Colin Moynihan, MP and Peter Baelz, Dean of Durham unveiling a plinth celebrating Durham Cathedral and Castle's UNESCO designation as a World Heritage Site, 1987.

universities were funded. The crucial factor was that teaching and research were to be funded separately. Teaching was provided for by a standard unit of resource across all universities, depending on the subject, whereas research funding was allocated selectively through the Research Assessment Exercise (RAE). This was a major change. In practice, teaching came first in the budget, with research receiving what was left.

When the settlement under the new system for 1985/86 to 1989/90 was announced, Durham was expected to make savings of more than 4 per cent every year. Since significant cuts had already been made over the previous five years, it was difficult to know where further savings would come from. The scale of the crisis prompted more than sixty graduates, Harold Evans among them, to call the first ever extraordinary meeting of Convocation, held on 4 November 1985, to voice their concern.

Holliday had already made a passionate case for Durham and for university education in general when responding to the UGC in 1984. 'The ideal of University education remains what it has always been: to promote, in an atmosphere of free enquiry, the search for new knowledge; to provide the minds of those we educate with the means of self-command and the ability to compare, discriminate and analyse . . . [these arguments] have been rightly used to rebut proposals

87 Council minutes, 20 March 1984.

Facing page, Gamma ray telescope, Physics at Work exhibition, 1991/2.

Engineering students, 1991. In 1838 Durham became the first university in Britain to run a course in engineering, with a programme in Civil and Mining Engineering.

including chairs, were left unfilled. The School of Oriental Studies was broken up. There were discussions between universities over the merger of departments and the shared use of facilities. In 1985 classics staff from Bangor transferred to Durham, and in 1987 a Joint Centre for East Asian Studies was formed with Newcastle. Student protests, marches and sit-ins, which had taken place regularly since 1979, became more frequent. Students feared the University was in danger of becoming nothing more than a college of science or technology. But still the Vice-Chancellor held on to his belief in Durham as a balanced collegiate university. *Palatinate* reported that 'a determination pervades [academic staff] that Durham should not primarily become a teaching university or a commercial enterprise and that everyone should stick together in their attempt to maintain a "balanced" university'.[88] So several departments were grouped together in new schools, such as the School of Modern European Languages, the School of Biological Sciences and the School of Engineering and Applied Sciences. Music, despite its small size, was deliberately maintained, not just because of its research reputation, but also because of the contribution it made to the community, both within and outside the University.

One incident illustrates just how fiercely Durham had to fight in defence of academic breadth and excellence. The UGC, recalled Fred Holliday, wanted Durham to close the geology department. For sixty years geology had represented intellectual excellence in Durham. The Vice-Chancellor refused point blank to accept the UGC's demand. He would not have resigned, but he left the possibility hanging in the air. Holliday emphasised to all those around him that the University was 'in the survival game'[89] and they could not be spared reality. 'Openness and mutual trust would be essential if morale was to be maintained', he told Council.[90] As letters flowed in from staff unhappy about the impact of cuts on their departments, the Vice-Chancellor asked the Senate 'for patience in the present difficult period'.[91] The Association of University Teachers was once provoked into taking action by poor pay settlements nationally imposed, but remained courteous and understanding of the University's plight.

The University had to keep so many different plates spinning at the same time that it was hardly surprising there were complaints. Students protested against rising maintenance fees. At Hatfield, for instance, students walked out of formal dinner and demonstrated outside the college gates. The University acknowledged the gap between what students could afford and what the colleges needed. But the Vice-Chancellor and college heads insisted that an increase was necessary for the survival of the colleges. Defending the

88 *Palatinate,* 14 May 1987.

89 Personal interview with Sir Fred Holliday, 6 December 2005.
90 Council minutes, 8 July 1986.
91 Senate minutes, 24 March 1987.

colleges was as vital for the future of the University as securing a balanced curriculum. Later, at least one college Principal reflected that the finely judged policy of the University had left the collegiate system largely untouched. It was clear that the Treasurer, Alec McWilliam, and his successor, Paulina Lubacz, were acting in the best interests of the University as a whole, and attempts were made to secure external funding.

The University's trouble was nothing compared with the turmoil that was affecting thousands of people throughout County Durham in the mid-1980s. The miners' strike of 1984–85 preceded the wholesale closure of coal mines throughout the country. It was the death knell for an industry that had filled the coffers of the diocese and so helped to found the University 150 years earlier, and for a way of life that had kept the county's heart beating for centuries. In 1984 the Bishop, David Jenkins, took the side of the miners and their families during a dispute that broke families in two and divided the country. Within the University, DSU, while concerned with the impact of education cuts on its members, also showed compassion for the miners, securing cheap food and other goods for them, and courting controversy with the University authorities (and the University Conservative Association) in the process. Simon Pottinger, president of DSU, organised a series of debates at Collingwood and recalled that 'a group of miners' wives spoke and they triumphed over serious opposition from some "rahs" on the back row'.[92] One of the women later told him that it was the first time she had spoken in public. A benefit concert was also held in Dunelm House. DSU's activities aroused the interest of Special Branch and there were rumours of phone-tapping and mail being intercepted. This expression of social concern was not a one-off. For some years, students and local people had been working together in a voluntary community service and action group, initially known as Folkus, helping the elderly, the disabled, the mentally ill and disadvantaged children.

Within the University the Vice-Chancellor always insisted that no matter how tough things got, Durham should cling to the highest aspirations. Part of such aspirations was to improve the level and quality of research in the University. Fred Holliday appreciated from the moment he took over as Vice-Chancellor that this would be a critical factor in attracting future funding. In Durham he found pockets of excellent research, especially among the science departments. Astronomy, for instance, traditionally but intermittently part of Durham, had become one of the strongest subjects in the country under the direction of the Professor of Experimental Physics, Arnold Wolfendale. In 1982 he persuaded Council to seek funds to revive the chair in astronomy. Thanks to the department's excellent reputation, Richard Ellis, one of the members of the cosmology group created by Wolfendale, and an international authority on observational cosmology, was appointed to the chair in 1985. A few years later, Wolfendale could write that 'the modern Durham astronomer flits between the optical, infra-red, ultra-violet, radio and X-ray wavebands. Gamma rays are entering the fold, neutrino astronomy is not far off, and the end of the century may see gravitational waves making their entrance, not to mention cosmic rays

92 *Durham First*, Autumn 1999.

A student working on a telescope in the Physics department, 2006. Durham has one of the world's leading departments specialising in Astronomy and Astrophysics. Its research group on galaxy evolution is the largest in Europe and it is a major user of the Hubble Space Telescope.

Graduation day.

finally becoming accepted'.[93] By then, Wolfendale's own reputation had earned him the position of Astronomer Royal in 1991. He retired from teaching in 1992 and was knighted in 1995.

Overall, however, the standard was patchy. Holliday wanted to find a way of promoting research throughout the University. The idea he came up with was the Durham University Research Foundation. It was funded partly from within existing budgets, thanks to the ingenuity of the University Treasurer, and partly from the proceeds of the University's 150th anniversary appeal. This had raised nearly £1.5 million and some of this was applied to the endowment of twenty research fellowships. The Foundation encouraged research not only within the University and between departments, but also through external associations. It succeeded in creating an academic atmosphere that, Holliday recalled, was 'hugely congenial'.[94]

Holliday knew from his own experience that a university was much stronger for being deeply rooted within the wider community. He also believed that regional links would be vital for the universities of the future. Yet he found Durham wrapped in cotton wool, largely insulated not just from the region, but from the local community. Holliday saw the University as an integral part of the region, something it had never been. The start of this was the University's partnership with English Industrial Estates, in 1982, to develop what became the Mountjoy Science Park. The park was intended to 'support the development of advanced technology research and development in the Northern Region'.[95] It was an astute move, in tune with government priorities and building on Durham's strength in the sciences. The site would include the University's own Centre for Materials Science and Technology, an initiative partly funded by appeal proceeds and one that was warmly welcomed by the Science and Engineering Research Council (SERC) for bringing academics and business closer together. It was probably also the first time that the strengths of individual departments had been pooled in one venture, in this case, applied physics and electronics, chemistry, engineering, geological sciences and the Business School.

Holliday found that this regional and local commitment could be furthered through existing avenues in the University, through the School of Education, the Business School and the Department of Continuing and Adult Education. The reaction was very positive – local councils and councillors, regional agencies and other bodies all asked why this had not been done before. A branch of the Business School was opened temporarily at Consett, in the wake of the closure of the steelworks and the end of the miners' strike, with the closure of so many pits in County Durham. This

93 Wolfendale, A W, *Durham and the New Astronomies*, DUJ, July 1992.
94 Holliday interview.
95 Council minutes, 2 November 1982.

made a valuable contribution to the economic revival of the area.

As well as regional relationships, Holliday was eager to develop overseas links. Previously, the international connections forged by the University had been with Fourah and Codrington Colleges. Holliday wanted to bring the world to Durham and take Durham out into the world. This had been part of the reason for creating the Office of Commercial and Public Affairs in the early 1980s. There was, recalled Holliday, 'a touch of the Shangri La about Durham'.[96] In a more competitive educational environment, this had to change. The University's choice of Chancellor to succeed Malcolm McDonald in 1982 was part of this process. Dame Margot Fonteyn, the greatest ballerina of the second half of the twentieth century, most famous for her thrilling stage relationship with Rudolf Nureyev, brought an international elegance and glamour to the University through her role as its principal ambassador. Dragging Durham onto the international stage was also the reason why the University hosted the Quinquennial Confer-

Ballerina Dame Margot Fonteyn de Arias, Chancellor 1981-91, brought her own stamp of glamour and elegance to the role. She was the first non-Royal female chancellor of a UK university.

ence of Rectors, Presidents and Vice-Chancellors of European Universities in 1989. The formal relationship with Teikyo University of Japan, agreed in the previous year, also 'epitomised Durham as a University with growing international links'.[97] Accommodation for Japanese students and staff adjacent to St Mary's College was opened by the Duchess of Kent on 24 April 1990.

The commitment to a regional role for the University became entwined with a wish to increase access, as the realisation dawned that it was too small for the changed circumstance of higher education in the UK. In 1987 there were just under 5,000 students at the University. Durham had to grow to make the most of its facilities, resources and income when the latter depended on less and less money per student. The UGC, shortly to be abolished, was now predicting that the late 1990s would see an upsurge in university students, but that this increase would have to be met by existing resources, supplemented with other sources of funding. Government now wanted universities to open their doors more widely.

Graduation day.

96 Holliday interview.
97 Council minutes, 24 May 1988.

Bearing in mind the potential to do so in the north-east, it was a clear indication that Durham needed to expand. The question was how this expansion could be achieved. If more students came to Durham, more accommodation, both residential and teaching, had to be provided.

The student population rose from 5,000 to 6,200 between 1987 and 1992, although the University was ill-equipped to absorb the extra numbers. Departments expanded rapidly as they sought economies of scale by recruiting more students per member of staff. As a result, the ratio of staff to students declined, small group teaching was threatened, the lack of teaching space became desperate and timetabling difficulties were common. The library and other student resources were overstretched. This influx of students also strained the college system and the capacity of the city of Durham to accommodate more students. By 1989 some colleges could no longer provide rooms for all their first-year students. It became common practice in many colleges for first-year ballots to be held to decide which freshers would have to live out. Priority for college

Evelyn Ebsworth, Vice-Chancellor 1990–98.

rooms was given to first- and third-years, although there was no guarantee even for them. JCRs protested that this would change the character of the colleges irrevocably. Some colleges decided that only first-year students could be allocated tutors because of the pressure of greater numbers. The tutorial system had long been subject to criticism and some now felt it needed to be overhauled completely. 'The creaking tutorial system, little more than a sad joke to most students, should be given a good kick up the arse.'[98] There were even those who advocated its abolition. But one college Principal, Victor Watts of Grey, pointed out that greater numbers and more students living out could very well increase the need for a revived tutorial system. In suggesting that tutoring was one of the features that helped to sustain Durham's colleges, he provided a succinct definition of a college as 'a community, academic and familial, of staff and students, young and old, crossing disciplinary boundaries'.[99]

Increased numbers within Durham did little to meet the challenge of welcoming a more diverse group of people into

Student life in the 1980s and 90s: *Clockwise from top left, Another Country*, produced by Bloody Hill Theatre Company, 1986; Charles Hardin, Hatfield College, 1991; Dunelm Arts Festival, Fats Jazz club, 1991; Launch of a new magazine, *Inside Out*, 1984; Tamzin Smith, 1986.

98 *Palatinate*, 12 October 1990.
99 *Palatinate*, 14 February 1991.

Castle dining room in the Great Hall.

the University. In 1989, 40 per cent of Durham's admissions still came from independent schools. The national average was 22 per cent. There was a perception, said some, that Durham was 'a beleaguered colonial outpost of Surrey stranded among a sea of Geordies'.[100]

However, Durham seized the opportunity to make a difference on its own doorstep. Teesside was close by; it had a huge population, it was under-provided with higher education, it had a potential pool of talent and it could also relieve the pressure on crowded Durham. The genesis of the idea for a new college was first expressed by Fred Holliday in 1987. His own experience at Stirling University had shown what could be done on a greenfield site. In the same year, Margaret Thatcher visited the derelict Head Wrightson Engineering Works on Teesside as part of the general election campaign. The point she was making was the need to regenerate parts of the country where traditional heavy industries had disappeared. She was accompanied by the Vice-Chancellor and told him that his idea could form a key part of a local regeneration scheme. Ron Norman and Duncan Hall, the chairman and chief executive of the Teesside Development Corporation, also expressed support, and talks began in earnest in 1988. Planning for the new college was entrusted to the Pro-Vice-Chancellor, James Barber, also Master of Hatfield. The plan was to make provision for 1,000 students by 1991. 'Our aim,' said Barber, 'is to widen access and to draw to Teesside those who would want to go to University but will now be able to remain in the area'.[101] This was a reversion to the idea of the university with strong local ties, as both Durham and Newcastle had been for many years. It was decided early on that the college would be developed in partnership with Teesside Polytechnic, a decision greeted with

Left, Jonathan Edwards read Physics at Van Mildert, 1984–87. His 1995 18.29m world record was the first ever 60 foot triple jump.

Below, left to right, Will Carling, at 22, was England's youngest rugby captain, 1988–96. He studied Psychology at Hatfield, 1985–88.

Nasser Hussain, read Natural Sciences at St Hild and St Bede's, 1986–89. England cricket captain 1999–2003.

Phillip de Glanville, read Economics and Politics at University College 1987-90. England rugby captain 1996–97.

Andrew Strauss, studied Economics at Hatfield, graduating in 1998. England cricket captain, 2006.

Will Greenwood, studied Economics at Hatfield, 1991-93. His two fondest memories are winning the Rugby World Cup, 2003 and his first year at Durham in 1990.

100 *Palatinate,* 24 June 1982.
101 *Palatinate,* 1 November 1988.

dismay by some members of the Senate, but regarded as essential in attracting new types of students to new types of courses. The intention was to combine teaching and research in subjects often new for Durham, and in a multidisciplinary manner alien to Durham's traditional departmental structure. Joint degrees were envisaged in health studies and nursing, human biology and human sciences, drama and theatre studies, as well as courses in education, environmental sciences, European studies and business management. The chosen location was the site of the same derelict engineering works in Stockton visited by Margaret Thatcher.

HM Queen Elizabeth II visited the University in 1991. On the right, Vice-Chancellor Evelyn Ebsworth.

The newly knighted Sir Fred Holliday handed over the project to his successor in 1990. It was an initiative warmly supported by the new Vice-Chancellor. Professor Evelyn Ebsworth, a graduate of King's College, Cambridge, had been Crum Brown Professor of Chemistry at Edinburgh University. A specialist in synthetic and structural chemistry, he had also acted as Dean of Sciences. He knew Durham from occasional lecture invitations. He liked the collegiate system because it created vibrant communities where people of different interests and disciplines mixed together. Durham, he found, was 'a place full of lively people'.[102]

Those lively people, sparking off each other, given freedom to express their talents and enthusiasm, were already producing on the stage, on the concert platform, in the debating chamber and on the playing field the excellence the University was seeking throughout Durham. Among the leading lights of the stage were James Wilby and Kevin Lygo. The outstanding athlete was Jonathan Edwards, who broke four records at the British University Athletics Championships in 1986. The University nurtured a number of talented cricketers, most notably Nasser Hussain, a member of the record-breaking 1987 1st XI that won three titles, the Reader Trophy and the McKechnie and Wishart Cups in the UAU championship. Hussain went on to captain the England side for forty-five Test matches between 1999 and 2003 – more than any other captain except Michael Atherton. He was also the third most successful captain,

Cicely Shaw, Castle porter, brandishing the Castle keys on her retirement, 1989.

behind Peter May and Mike Brearley, with seventeen victories. Durham rugby players from the period who went on to national honours included Mark Bailey, Will Carling, Chris Oti and Phil de Glanville. The DUBC continued to shine at the highest levels, winning a string of UAU titles, while the Durham University Women's Boat Club also gained in strength, confidence and success. Other notable champions included the lacrosse, hockey, swimming, orienteering and golf teams.

The new Vice-Chancellor, who supported the idea for a new college in Durham as well as in Stockton, was less sure about the overall direction of the University. To discuss this he gathered together an informal group of academic staff, those long-established and others more recently arrived. Their views helped to formulate the paper, Durham 2000, approved by the Senate at the end of 1991, that set the strategy for the University over the next decade. Given the expectation of government that universities would continue to expand, driving down costs as they did so, it was felt that Durham, with Stockton, might see numbers rise to 10,000 by the year 2000. A quarter of that increase would be in Durham, which made a new college essential. The value of the collegiate system as the essence of Durham was reinforced. It was important to build on the achievements of the previous decade by aiming for all-round excellence, based on high-calibre staff and students. Academic developments would be driven by research centres, there would be greater support for postgraduates and research, and every encouragement would be given to departments to create stronger relationships with international institutions. Involvement with commerce and industry locally and regionally would be deepened. Attracting outside funding would be of paramount importance for achieving many of these goals, making closer relations with alumni of the University essential.

When University College, Stockton, opened with 190 students in October 1992, it was the first new college in the University for twenty years, and the first outside Durham. Stockton heralded an exciting and radical new chapter in the University's history.

102 Personal interview with Evelyn Ebsworth, 9 November 2005.

Shaped by the Past, Creating the Future: from 1992

THE 1990s WAS THE DECADE WHEN the University of Durham began to blossom as never before. Financial challenges, although never as acute as those of the 1980s, remained a fact of life, not just for Durham, but for every institute of higher education in the UK. This was no longer a surprise, however, but something the University could plan for. So now it could turn its energies towards building on the foundations which had already been laid down for wider access, extended research and a truly international profile. Durham was ready to take to a wider audience than ever before the special experience born of more than 150 years deeply rooted in one of the world's most outstanding cultural, architectural and historically important places. What Durham had to offer was a vision of a broadly based seat of learning, founded on excellence in teaching and research, with an expanding international reputation, playing a vital role within the region, and offering life-changing opportunities to young people of all backgrounds.

Evelyn Ebsworth, the Vice-Chancellor, never wavered from this vision during his term of office. Neither did his successor, although Sir Kenneth Calman, who took over the post in 1998, was a very different man. A graduate in biochemistry and medicine, he had spent fifteen years as a professor at Glasgow University, first of oncology and then of postgraduate medical education. He then became Chief

Students at the Castle.

Medical Officer at the Scottish Office before moving in 1991 to become Chief Medical Officer at the Department of Health. Here he reorganised cancer services in England, and played a major part in the redevelopment of postgraduate medical education. Over a decade and a half, these two very different men ensured that their shared vision transformed the University of Durham.

The 1990s heralded a very different era for British universities. They were encouraged to recruit more and more students, reaching out to young people who would never have considered taking up a place at university. But they were also encouraged to become more responsible for their own finances. There never was enough government money to finance this almost unprecedented expansion in numbers. Between the early 1990s and 2001 the proportion of young people in the UK eligible to study at university rose from less than 20 per cent to 33 per cent. Reminiscent of the 1960s, this represented an increase of more than two million young men and women. Durham's numbers, including those at Stockton, more than doubled. More students compelled the UGC's successor, the Higher Education Funding Council for England (HEFCE), to cut revenue and capital grants for universities in order to make the money go round. Faced with this, even the ingenuity of university finance directors could not overcome the problem of constantly trying to do more with less. Eventually, tuition fees and a system of student loans repaid from income on graduation were introduced. From September 2006, every new student at Durham, as at most other universities, was faced with annual tuition fees of £3,000. This impending prospect made it important to ensure that, as far as possible, every student with the ability to come to Durham was not deterred from doing so because of their financial circumstances.

Almost all students, undergraduates and postgraduates, depend on financial support from one source or another to see them through their courses. Even before the introduction of tuition fees, there were tales of students with maximum loans taking two jobs, working twenty-four hours a week to make ends meet; of students from disadvantaged backgrounds struggling even with part-time jobs to pay the rent. In the year 2000, 10 per cent of students at Durham applied for financial aid, a 30 per cent increase on the previous year. Two years later, one calculation was that Durham's students were £16 million in debt. The University's Student Opportunities Fund, which also helps to fund important extras such as expeditions and travel, became more and more important. It now plays a crucial part in sustaining the traditional breadth of the University's vision. The Student Opportunities Fund reached more than £1 million in 2003, thanks to generous donations from Durham graduates. This support has become even more vital under the new system of student loans and tuition fees, with limited student finances stretched by increasing residence charges for the colleges, and with Durham seeking to attract more students from less privileged circumstances. Part of the University's 175th anniversary appeal is devoted to endowing more scholarships and bursaries.

At the same time, successive governments insisted that more and more university funding should be tied to the standard of teaching and research. The higher the standards, the better the funding. Durham took on this challenge as well, confident in the ability of University staff to meet the increasingly rigorous standards demanded. These came through the Research Assessment Exercise (RAE), which governed a university's status and eligibility for research grants; and the Teaching Quality Assessment (TQA), administered by yet another acronym, the QAA, or Quality Assurance Agency, charged with monitoring university teaching and educational standards.

Finding money from sources other than government became more vital than ever. UK universities began to recognise the financial value of keeping in touch with their alumni, attracting sponsorship for new ventures, raising a little bit of extra income by approving credit cards promoted to their graduates. Durham was no exception. There were sponsored chairs, such as the Allen & Overy chair in European law, established in 1994. A major donation from the Sultan of Sharjah, a Durham graduate, funded new premises for the Centre for Islamic and Middle Eastern Studies in 1996. Sponsorship was especially critical for minority subjects (as they were classed), which lacked the critical mass driving the expansion of major subjects. And success bred success. In 1997 the University's outstanding reputation for science, based on the track record of the departments of chemistry and physics, particularly, attracted a generous donation from Dr (later Sir) Peter Ogden, a graduate of the University and founder of Computacenter. This helped to launch what became the Ogden Centre for Fundamental Physics, specialising in computational cosmology, that is, the structure of the universe, and particle physics phenomenonology, or the investigation of the smallest elementary particles. It was eventually opened by Baroness Greenfield in 2002.

The University's Development Office recognised that fund-raising was becoming more competitive among universities and Durham could not lag behind. In 1997–98 telephone fund-raising, using current students, brought in £350,000. In the same period, other private donations contributed almost £1.7 million. In 1999, the 1832 Society was formed for the University's most generous donors. Eventually, in 2005, the post of Director of Development and Communications was created, with the appointment of Liesl Elder from the USA, to drive forward the fund-raising effort and to work on alumni relations.

103 Tuck, A, *Collingwood College, University of Durham – A Jubilee History 1972–1997*, Durham, 1997, p. 110.

The Ogden Centre for Fundamental Physics. Named after the benefactor and businessman and Durham physics graduate Professor Sir Peter Ogden, it is a world-leading centre of excellence in fundamental physics research. It was opened in 2002 by Prime Minister Tony Blair who admitted that he was a poor physics student at school.

But not everything the University did could hope to attract external funding. When every penny counted, it was almost inevitable that finance would become further centralised. The complaints were also inevitable, particularly from the colleges. One college Principal wrote that 'the degree of financial control from the centre now gives [the colleges] little real say over how they spend their money'.[103] Expected to finance loans for any new building from future income generated by that building, their finances were in a parlous position. The colleges too realised how much more important other sources of income had become. This essentially meant maximising revenue from vacation conferences. Almost all the new additions to existing colleges were built with their attraction to the conference trade in mind. But the colleges were also turning to their alumni and other donors to raise funds for otherwise unaffordable improvements. Several colleges had already formed their own trusts, such as Hatfield in 1987 and Grey in 1990.

College maintenance was another challenge. In 1993, to help with maintenance, students were charged a building levy for the first time, starting at £35 per student and rising to £140 within four years. This was obviously unpopular when students were having to supplement inadequate grants with loans. And they had already been complaining about overcrowded lecture rooms, an unsatisfactory library, the shabby state of the University's squash courts, the antiquated running track and outdated facilities at Maiden Castle. There was also the spectre of a collapsing Castle once again. An extensive programme of repairs had to be abandoned in the 1990s because of a lack of funds, even though the building's position as part of a world heritage site gave access to funds Percy Heawood and his colleagues could only have dreamt of in the 1920s. It was only in 2004 that a generous donation from the Northern Rock Foundation, matched by the University, enabled the commencement of the first phase in a long-term project estimated to cost £7 million.

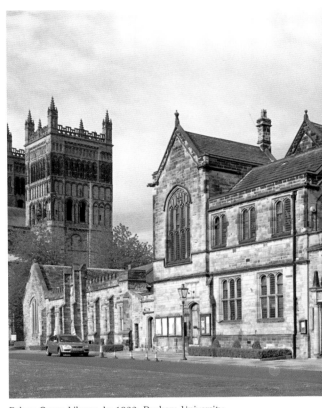

Palace Green Library. In 1833, Durham University Library was established on Palace Green with a collection of 160 volumes donated by William Van Mildert, co-founder of the University.

The Science Library was expanded in 1983 to become the University's main library. The University Library now has more than 1.5 million printed works, manuscripts and archives, as well as online and electronic resources.

103 Tuck, A, *Collingwood College, University of Durham – A Jubilee History 1972–1997*, Durham, 1997, p. 110.

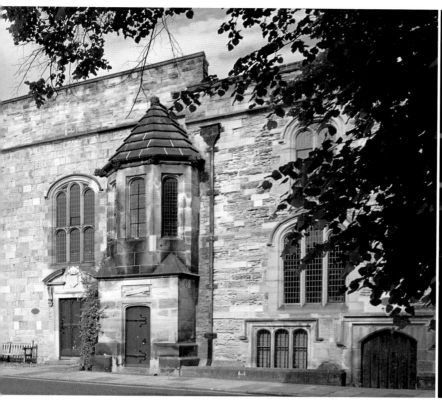

Palace Green Library houses resources for Law, Music and Local History and is also the main base for the Archives and Special Collections.

The University Treasurer, Paulina Lubacz, and her staff did a remarkable and often under-appreciated job in guiding the University through a difficult period. Despite constraints, they succeeded in financing several important new buildings in Durham in the early 1990s. The University recognised that much of its teaching and research accommodation was no longer adequate. The chemistry department, for one, was having to turn down research projects because of lack of space. Research grants as yet covered only direct project costs and provided nothing for overheads or infrastructure. An extension was added to the physics building, and in 1994 the department of biological sciences moved into the largest science building constructed within the University for thirty years. An extension was built for the University's Business School. The chemistry department was refurbished, as well as the Dawson Building, where a home was created on the science site for the University's outstanding archaeology department. Plans were also implemented for a much needed extension to the central library, although budget cuts forced the closure of several departmental libraries.

Perhaps the most ambitious project managed by the University during the 1990s was the development of the campus at Stockton. Officially opened by the Queen on 18 May 1993, Stockton would become a beacon of Durham's determination to offer the accumulated advantages of its learning to a broader social range of potential students. But its early years were not easy. Limited finances meant that it was run on a shoestring, with limited courses, insufficient staff and underdeveloped facilities. In Stockton the initial dropout rate was more than double that in the rest

of the University. The go-ahead was given to proceed with the first student residences in January 1994, just as government policy changed, halting the rush for growth in student places which had underpinned Stockton's financial viability.

It was now that the two partners, Durham and Teesside, agreed that Durham would assume financial and administrative responsibility for the campus. This was actually the precursor of the ultimate and amicable withdrawal of Teesside University from the project. University College, Stockton, or UCS, effectively became part of the University of Durham. When Professor Parfitt retired as the first Principal in April 1994, his place was taken by Durham's Registrar, John Hayward, later Stockton's first Provost. His efforts proved central to steering Stockton back on course and forward to success. New programmes were introduced, research became a priority and more effort was put into recruiting a wider range of students (almost half of all entrants came from non-traditional backgrounds). The first hall of residence was opened by the Earl of Stockton in 1995, with 230 en-suite rooms, although other communal facilities remained very limited. The campus began to specialise in environmental, human and biomedical sciences, plus education, including teacher training. A little later, more subjects were added, including applied psychology, sports science, business finance and urban studies. An early research initiative, the Research Centre in Reactor Engineering, was formed in partnership with local industry, through Davy Process Technology (later Kvaerner). In 1995 the first graduates received their degrees in Stockton parish church from the Chancellors of the two Universities, Sir Peter Ustinov, who had succeeded Dame Margot Fonteyn, and Lord Brittan, the former Home Secretary.

Over the next few years, UCS continued to grow, reaching nearly 1,000 students by 1997/98. As well as the addition of more courses, including collaboration between Durham and Newcastle on a joint degree in medical science, the research side of UCS was developed further. The Teesside Development Corporation, in its final year, granted UCS £800,000 to establish a chair and research centre in regional regeneration and development studies, linked to the University's outstanding geography department. There were also plans, as part of the University's commitment to opening its doors to potential students from different backgrounds, to create a Centre for Lifelong Learning for the promotion of part-time degrees, but this fell by the wayside. The progress made by UCS since its opening was highlighted by the report of the QAA in May 1998, which concluded that through excellent management and leadership, and the commitment of students and staff, the University's work at Stockton 'has served to enhance the academic reputation of the University',[104] an indisputable riposte to the patronising carping of some who had seen Stockton as a threat to Durham's academic standing. The University's continued commitment to UCS was seen in the largest single building project it had ever carried out. Opened at the end of 1998, the Ebsworth Building comprised a second teaching and learning facility and 200 en-suite student rooms.

In the same year, Teesside finally withdrew from the college, whose students now took their degrees entirely within the University of Durham. The teaching and learning facilities at UCS, which now became known as the University of Durham Stockton Campus, were second to none in the University, and its research base was growing, with plans for another major research building. A £15 million programme was planned for doubling the size of the college

Renowned raconteur, Sir Peter Ustinov never failed to entertain, as here with Lady Evelyn Barbirolli. He was an 'outstanding friend and ambassador to the University' (Sir Kenneth Calman, Vice-Chancellor).

104 Hayward, J, *Breaking the Mould – The Surprising Story of Stockton*, unpublished typescript, 1999, p. 77.

Sir Peter Ustinov, writer, director, UNICEF ambassador, wit and humanitarian, was the tenth Chancellor of the University. After his inauguration in 1992 he awarded honorary doctorates to Glenda Jackson, the actor and politician and Terry Waite, the Archbishop of Canterbury's envoy, who was held hostage in Beirut.

John Snow College at Queen's Campus, Stockton, founded in 2001, named after the public health pioneer.

George Stephenson College, also founded at Queen's Campus in 2001, named after the great railroad engineer.

Railway pioneer George Stephenson, inventor of the Rocket steam locomotive for the Stockton and Darlington Railway which became the first to carry passenger traffic. Sculpture by Colin Wilbourne, for 'In the shadow of the past', Durham Botanic Gardens. He used wood from trees that were felled because they had Dutch elm disease.

to 2,000 students. Yet recruitment into the campus's original courses and of mature students was falling away, while the organisation of 1,000 students as one college ran counter to the tradition within Durham of relatively small colleges with distinctive identities. The question of the next few years, as Stockton continued to expand, would be how best to integrate it within the University as a whole.

The idea of the colleges as an intrinsic part of the University, yet individually distinctive, was partly behind the drive to integrate properly Stockton within the University. In May 2000, Adrian Darnell, the Vice-Provost responsible for student services at Stockton, suggested creating two new colleges, on the Durham model, as a solution to the strain placed on pastoral support and the identity of the campus by increasing numbers. They would allow smaller groups to establish their own identities, lead to better pastoral care, help new students to settle in more quickly, provide a focus for social and other activities and create a greater bond with the wider University.

The new colleges came into being from September 2001. They were named after two great north-eastern figures, George Stephenson, one of the founders of the railways, and John Snow, the public health pioneer. The University still has to invest in the communal and sporting facilities which are so important to the identity of a college but everything else is there and the Principals of the two colleges have remarked on the enthusiasm among the students to engage in and create a true collegiate experience.

Integration within the University as a whole continued after the retirement of John Hayward in 2002, when the post of Provost was absorbed within the Vice-Chancellor's role. This was also the year when Stockton was renamed the Queen's Campus, following the visit of the Duke of Edinburgh; and when, for the first time, every student throughout the University graduated in the Norman splendour of Durham Cathedral. Stockton, with 3,000 students, is the same size as Durham was in the 1970s.

In 2002 another landmark for Stockton occurred, confirming its potential as a future powerhouse of research within the University, when the Wolfson Institute was opened by Baroness Greenfield. Focused on medicine, health and the environment, this could not have been accomplished without the generous donation of £4 million from the Wolfson Foundation, another example of the importance of funding from outside the usual sources. Ray Hudson, who had helped to build geography into the leading department in the country, with experience of organising high quality research, was appointed as director of the Institute, aiming to give it greater direction and energy. He intended to extend the influence of the Institute across the university, across disciplines and beyond other boundaries. The example in interdisciplinary research set by the Wolfson Institute later influenced the University's proposal for an Institute of Advanced Studies.

This in turn has fostered the involvement of the University in the region, with a programme aimed at improving the health and well-being of the local community, making links at every level, from

Psychology Department.

Watersports at Queen's Campus, Stockton.

general practices to regional development organisations. This was yet another step forward in raising the University's regional profile. During the 1990s this had already been strengthened through the work of the Business School. A number of partnerships aimed at furthering regional wealth generation were established with Newcastle University. These had included the North East Centre for Micro Electronics and the Regional Centre for Electronics and Technology. Durham also expanded the Mountjoy Science Park, with local businesses in the vanguard of technological development. As Evelyn Ebsworth had noted in 1993, 'collaboration with industry and the use of science in the creation of wealth was part of the University's ethos'.[105] For Kenneth Calman, ten years later, this type of initiative represented the practical implementation of his vision of the University as a channel for delivering the common good.

The clear success of the University's involvement in Stockton contrasted with the struggle to open a new college in Durham itself. By 1993, second-year students were being squeezed out of college accommodation because of the pressure of numbers. This was a worsening situation, with an additional 1,500 students expected to come to Durham over the next few years. More accommodation was already planned at Collingwood, Grey, Van Mildert, St Mary's and St Aidan's. A new college was desperately needed to reduce the gap.

Plans for the new college, located at Howlands Farm, south of Collingwood, and intended to house 600 students, were slowed down by financing problems. A design competition was held, but the winning submission by Arup proved to be too expensive. Even when it was modified, the costs, including the major expense of providing infrastructure on a greenfield site, still totalled £20 million, of which £8 million had to be found from external sources. Planning consent for the new college was granted in 1994, but three years later a start had still not been made. In the meantime, government grants for new buildings were savagely cut back, other applications for funding had been turned down and only slow progress was being made in raising the money from elsewhere. This was partly why the University eventually decided to postpone plans for the college and embarked on a smaller project to improve accommodation for graduate students.

If it wanted to expand and enhance its research activities, the University needed to attract more graduate students. The Graduate Society had for years been complaining that postgraduates were the poor relations in the University. So the University reviewed the progress of the new college. It had always been intended that this would be linked with a new research institute. The completed building, with accommodation for 200 graduates, was opened at Howlands by the Duke of York in 2000. Three years later, the Graduate Society became Ustinov College, named after the University's Chancellor, with more than 1,000 students from seventy countries. Sir Peter Ustinov, presiding at the inauguration of the College, emphasised that 'there is nothing that can replace the contact of young people of different nations in contributing to a world at peace and freedom from ugly prejudice.'[106]

Durham became more and more successful in attracting international students to the University during the 1990s. The University's International Office created several links with universities overseas, from the USA and Russia to China and Japan. Today Durham welcomes postgraduate students from a staggering 120 countries. It is investing in improved support and supervision, regarding all this as an inherent

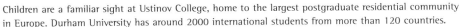

Children are a familiar sight at Ustinov College, home to the largest postgraduate residential community in Europe. Durham University has around 2000 international students from more than 120 countries.

105 Council minutes, 6 July 1993.
106 *Durham First*, Spring 2003.

part of the University's ethos. The competition for the twenty doctoral fellowships awarded by the University every year is intense, illustrating just how much the most talented graduate students from all over the world want to come to Durham.

An invaluable role in promoting Durham nationally and internationally was played by Sir Peter Ustinov, the University's Chancellor from 1992 until his death in 2004. His energy and commitment were remarkable, presiding over countless degree ceremonies, often in trying conditions, with unflagging good humour. His graduation speeches were unforgettable for those who heard them. On one occasion, after the University had moved the ceremony from the Castle to the Cathedral in 2002 because of rising numbers, he heard a baby cry in the audience. The rest of his speech was an impromptu exercise in baby talk that brought the house down. He was held in great affection and respect, which was compounded by the easy manner he had with everyone he met.

But the creation of Ustinov College did little to ease the accommodation crisis for the colleges or their students, or the increasing pressure on the city. The problems associated with any university town or city were magnified in Durham because there were so many more students in a small place, with many of them living outside college. Drunken rowdiness led at one point to the closure for three nights of all the college bars along the Bailey. One incident of excess involved the so-called Dun Cow Challenge, which involved downing ten pints of assorted lagers, beers and ciders in less than two hours.

Increasing numbers, without a new college, was placing the existing colleges under great strain. While there were plans to recreate the spirit of the colleges in Stockton, the tradition in Durham itself was feeling the pressure. By 1996, for instance, there were 920 students in Collingwood, of whom 40 per cent were living out. Communal facilities at Collingwood were overloaded, while links with nearly half the college were distant and more formal. Nevertheless, the colleges remained the vibrant heart of the University, and one of the most attractive aspects of Durham for prospective students. The Deputy Dean of Colleges described them in 1997 as 'a long-running success story. The colleges were lively academic

Ustinov College is the third largest college of Durham University. Founded as the Graduate Society it became a college in 2003 and was named after one of the university's chancellors, the late Sir Peter Ustinov.

Below left, Princess Diana bridge, Queen's Campus Stockton.

Below, playing pool at Ustinov College.

University Chancellor and author Bill Bryson, visits freshers at newly-opened Josephine Butler College, 2006.

communities conducting admissions to the University, providing libraries, fellowships, pastoral facilities and a wide range of opportunities for sporting and cultural activities for students. The question was how to continue this enhanced student experience, so important for attracting high calibre students'.[107] This was inevitably linked with ensuring that the experience was not diminished by Durham's expansion, and that the underinvestment in existing colleges was remedied.

From the moment he arrived as Vice-Chancellor in 1998, Kenneth Calman was eager to try to provide more students with rooms in college. The University's biggest residential project was eventually launched in 2004, when a design team was appointed for a £36 million, 400-bed college, which, along with 400 additional beds at Ustinov College and another 200 for St Cuthbert's Society at Parsons Fields, would add 1,000 places. In 2006 the new college opened as Butler College, named after Josephine Butler, the cousin of the reforming Earl Grey and an early advocate of women's

education in the north of England. Butler will relieve some of the pressure on accommodation in Durham, and was backed by the city which sees the collegiate system as alleviating housing pressures and providing better student support. It will leave half of all students with college accommodation. By reducing the proportion of freshers from more than 60 per cent in some colleges to less than 50 per cent, it will also create a more balanced collegiate community. Another change was the decision for St Mary's to admit men from 2005 – the last college in Durham to go mixed.

Community relations have also been helped by the University's involvement in local sport. These have been developed through Dr Peter Warburton, himself a Durham graduate and Bursar at Hild-Bede, who returned to the University as director of sport in 1995. The links with the city are numerous, through the swimming, cricket, rugby, hockey and fencing clubs. Players from the university take part in city teams, University and city coaches pool their resources, and about 200 students coach in the community. Three full-

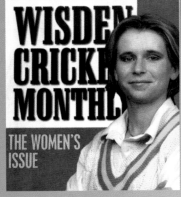

107 Council minutes, 27 May 1997.

time development officers, externally funded, work with all the county schools. There are weekly sports festivals at Maiden Castle, a major annual fun run and a charity rugby match before Christmas. This has been a catalyst for better working relationships. And, says Peter Warburton, 'it is the most exciting thing we do'.[108] These links stretch out across the region. There is a continuing project with rehabilitating drug addicts, working through football at both Stockton and Durham, and through fencing and trampolining at Durham. There are links with the Wear Valley sports action zone and the Easington education action zone. In 2005, young people from across Europe attended a summer school camp at Durham as part of the Year of the Child. Durham sends six talented athletes every year to Zambia, where the Zambian Sports Development Team works with local schools through sport to tackle HIV-Aids.

Community has been just one part of Durham's strategy for sport. Participation and performance have been the other two prongs. The University has maintained its outstanding record for student partic-

Josephine Butler College, known as 'Butler', is the first fully en-suite, self-catering college in Durham. It opened in 2006 and was named after the Victorian health pioneer and women's advocate.

Below from facing page, Isabelle Duncan, Durham graduate and first women to appear on the front cover of *Wisden,* the cricket magazine; cross country running; cricket; Durham Boat Race crew, 1998; Fencing; Durham University Hockey Team, winners of the 2006/7 BUSA Premiership.

108 Personal interview with Dr Peter Warburton, 6 December 2005.

ipation in sport (over 90 per cent) and today has a greater proportion of its students taking part in sport than any other UK university. New sports have multiplied, such as lacrosse for men and mixed teams, archery and even ultimate Frisbee. A massive part of this growth has been in women's sport, particularly in soccer and rugby, as well as more traditional female sports such as netball and hockey. There is, according to Peter Warburton, one main reason for this remarkable development. 'We have the fantastic structure of the colleges here which just makes everything work.'[109]

Sporting success has come from investment in full-time coaches in the five key sports – cricket, hockey, fencing, rugby and rowing. These target sports have as their ultimate objective the creation of world-class athletes playing for their country. But other sports are also encouraged to aim for world-class status, including mountaineering, canoeing, women's lacrosse and sailing. To minimise the tension between study and sport, the University has its own strength and conditioning team, devising individual programmes for talented sportspeople, as well as a sports psychologist. There are obstacles, usually physical ones – the University rows on the Tyne, but does not have a boathouse on the river; the women's tennis players have to use Sunderland courts; the netball teams play in Gateshead. Some refurbishment was carried out at Maiden Castle in 2001, and the running track, AstroTurf and tennis courts were upgraded. A multimillion pound indoor sporting facility for the University is

109 Warburton interview.

Durham Women's Rowing Four celebrating victory over Newcastle, 1997.

An Eight approaching Prebends Bridge.

Universities in an almighty row! Durham and Newcastle University Boat Clubs compete each year on the Tyne in the Northumbrian Water University Boat Race, 2003. The first race took place in 1997.

planned for 2008. All this success does not come cheaply, but the University's graduates have been consistently generous.

The list of titles won in recent years is almost endless, covering a wide cross-section of team and individual sports. In 2004 Durham recorded a triple crown unique in university sporting history, by simultaneously holding the university championships for cricket, rugby and rowing. In 2005 the University was ranked fifth overall in the British Universities Sports Association (BUSA) league tables, confirming its outstanding reputation in sport. Durham boasts one of only six university cricket Centres of Excellence and the team was granted first-class status in 2001. It is also an Amateur Rowing Association World Class Talent Centre. Outstanding individual athletes have included cricketers Caroline Atkins, James Foster (who was called up to play for England while still an undergraduate) and Andy Strauss, a member of the famous 2005 Ashes winning England side and then the England captain in 2006; rugby players Will Greenwood, who played in England's World Cup side, Tim Stimpson and Charlie Hodgson; swimmer Caroline Saxby; and rowers Wade Hall-Craggs and Peter Rudge.

Durham's students are also active in almost every other sphere. Most of them can take part in some activity at college or University level, particularly drama and music. Art is flourishing in the colleges. In the late 1990s, for instance, it was estimated that there was a public art exhibition almost every day of the year in the University,

Many of the Durham Colleges have modern art collections. St Aidan's College has a fine collection of work by Dame Elisabeth Frink, shown here in 1992 with one of her sculptures.

most of them held in the colleges. Many colleges have their own collections. St Aidan's, for example, has a fine collection of drawings and paintings by Elisabeth Frink, Norman Cornish and Douglas Pittuck, among others. The largest and most coherent collection of modern art in the University probably belongs to Trevelyan, with abstract canvasses by John Walker, as well as paintings by Mary Fedden and Julian Trevelyan. Grey College too has a contemporary collection, featuring works by artists such as John Piper, Thetis Blacker, Mary Cookson, Fay Pomerance and Birtley Aris.

The funds raised by Durham students for charity increase year by year. In 2005/06, for instance, almost £200,000 was presented to various charities and community projects, thanks to the activities organised through DUCK. In 2006, fifteen students, who had raised some £30,000, travelled to Sri Lanka to work with a community devastated by the tsunami disaster of 2004. The University was involved in helping with the reconstruction of the country through Project Sri Lanka, a partnership formed of staff and students, community and regional bodies. The students sent out in 2006 were

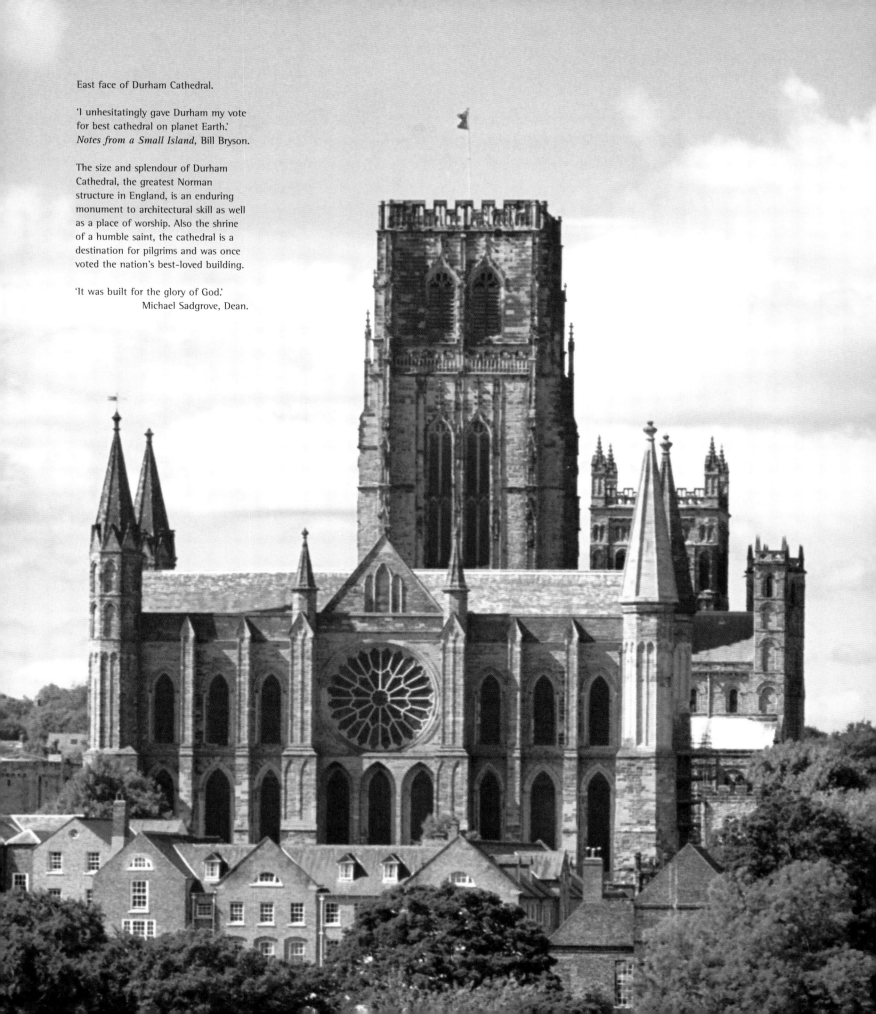

East face of Durham Cathedral.

'I unhesitatingly gave Durham my vote for best cathedral on planet Earth.'
Notes from a Small Island, Bill Bryson.

The size and splendour of Durham Cathedral, the greatest Norman structure in England, is an enduring monument to architectural skill as well as a place of worship. Also the shrine of a humble saint, the cathedral is a destination for pilgrims and was once voted the nation's best-loved building.

'It was built for the glory of God.'
Michael Sadgrove, Dean.

concerned with establishing a new school and providing new fishing boats as one part of the project. It provides a vivid demonstration of the University's international commitments.

As *Palatinate* noted in 2004, 'Durham's biggest strength is that it is full of people who care about a huge variety of different things, from college bars to heckling on the sidelines of sports matches . . . Durham students deserve credit in their own right for defining this university as the best place to get involved'.[110] In 2005, all this contributed to a student experience that recorded a satisfaction rate of 72.5 per cent in the National Students Survey, the fifth highest among British universities where a full range of degree courses was on offer, helping Durham to achieve recognition as the Sunday Times University of the Year. Durham also has the third highest rate for the completion of degrees, at 98 per cent of all students.

Students were also becoming more demanding of the standards they expected from their university. They were investing a great deal of effort simply in achieving a university place in a much more competitive environment, and then accruing significant personal debts in securing their degrees. The quality of teaching, already under constant scrutiny from government, was also being continually appraised by students. Durham generally performed extremely well in the teaching assessments carried out by the QAA. In 1995, for instance, eight of eleven departments assessed were judged excellent, the remainder satisfactory. Subsequent reviews would confirm the excellent quality of teaching in Durham.

Sir Kenneth Calman,
Vice-Chancellor, 1998–2007.

The University, learning lessons pioneered under John Hayward in Stockton, responded well to the shift towards the concept of teaching as facilitating learning. The University sought the views of recent graduates as well as current students, and developed new methods of teaching and assessment. The biggest single revolution came through the use of web-based teaching and learning materials, via the Durham University Online system (DUO). This began as a pilot scheme in 2000, and through staff enthusiasm and student demand became available to every student in departments and colleges within three years. In 2003 the University adopted the Blackboard Community System to enhance this expanding online system, covering not only academic requirements, but also community, society and sports sites, with links to banking services, bookstores and the University calendar. So students can use the system for everything from information about their classes to news about the latest college social events and paying bills online. It has become a 24-hour information network.

For the University, it was perhaps the enhancement of research standards that was most important. After the cuts of the 1980s, and under continued financial constraints thereafter, this was not easy. For the 1996 RAE, Durham's submission drew on the vision of a broadly based University, championed throughout the 1980s and 1990s. 'Some universities had concentrated substantial funds in a few areas whereas Durham had sought to support a wide spectrum of research'.[111] The results were mixed. A third of departments

Tony Blair opening the Sports Development Office, 1995.

Gordon Brown at Hild Bede College with
John Hayward and Kenneth Calman.

110 *Palatinate*, 7 October 2004.
111 Council minutes, 5 November 1996.

Durham University students have a strong history of activism.

received the highest grade, grade five, with the most outstanding performance coming from the geography department, awarded a starred grade five. But, as Professor Ebsworth reported, there were some 'unfortunate aspects',[112] and the University needed to re-emphasise the aims it had set itself several years earlier of improving standards in all departments.

The RAE scheduled for 2001 would obviously be critical for Durham. For Evelyn Ebsworth's successor, Sir Kenneth Calman, this was all bound up with the wider question of just what sort of university Durham wanted to be. In particular, he felt there was a need for a clearer strategic view of how Durham was going to achieve its ambition of all-round excellence. The University was still small compared with others, like UCL, Imperial and Manchester. A university of Durham's size, with ambitions to be among the top five universities in the UK, would have to focus on what it did best.

The immediate challenge was boosting research standards in anticipation of the 2001 RAE. This clearly required financial investment. The University began to use its academic reputation to bring in funds from government and elsewhere so a start could be made on the necessary improvements. In 1999, for example, the University extended the chemistry department in Durham by securing an award of more than £5 million from the government. In the following year, a grant of £9 million helped to create Europe's leading phenomenology centre for research into

the structure of the universe. More than £1 million came for a science enterprise centre. In 2001 Durham was awarded funding, jointly with Newcastle, to begin a course in preclinical medicine at Stockton. At the same time, successful bids for new money from HEFCE created additional student places in subjects like biological sciences, computer science, history and law. As a result, research teams housed in improved facilities won funding for new research projects, while more students on new courses brought in more income. Above all, the rewards were seen in the results of the 2001 RAE. Every department (bar one) achieved grade four or above. Six departments – chemistry, engineering, mathematics, geography, history and law – were awarded starred grade fives. For the Business School, the odd one out, the result acted as a stimulus to improvement. Within four years it had claimed the title of business school of the year from a prestigious European business journal.

The challenge remained, however, that superb results in standards of teaching and research brought very little extra direct funding. And Durham was becoming a victim of its increasing success. More teaching and residential buildings were needed because the University was attracting more students. By 2005 there would be 14,000 students in the University, 11,000 in Durham and 3,000 in Stockton. The University's most prestigious departments would only continue to be successful if the University carried on investing in them. The core budget was under intense strain.

112 Council minutes, 18 February 1997.

Leon Davico, right, receiving his honorary DCL at Sir Peter Ustinov's
installation as chancellor in the cathedral on 7 May 1992.

The Vice-Chancellor was certain that difficult decisions would need to be made, although he was full of almost boundless confidence that Durham would emerge stronger from the process. In the two years following the RAE, Durham took the necessary tough decisions. Fundamental changes were made to the way the University operated. Restructuring yielded major recurring savings, while the reform of senior management ensured that the use of these funds was supervised effectively.

In 2002 the 'super-deans' arrived. They were an important step forward in achieving the necessary compromise between striving for consensus and responding effectively to rapid change. The deans were given far greater executive powers, increasing their authority and influence within the faculties, with the faculty boards feeding in their views and opinions. Much larger faculties, bringing together schools and departments, were created. So, for instance, the Dean of Social Sciences and Health is responsible for 600 staff, 5,000 students and a budget of £42 million. The 'super-deans' went a long way to relieving the pressures on the University's central administration in Old Shire Hall. One reason for their enhanced credibility was that each of them had a place on another new body, the University Executive Committee, chaired by the Vice-Chancellor.

The same positive approach was taken with the colleges, seeking to minimise the previous sense of isolation they had felt from the centre, while capitalising on the enormous fund of goodwill within the colleges towards the University. The appointment of the Dean of Colleges to the University Executive Committee was hugely significant, recognising the central importance of the colleges. The Dean of Colleges was also given responsibility for the colleges' central budget. This helped to make the most of the resources available, through centralised purchasing, for instance, while maintaining the distinct character of each college.

As part of the management reorganisation, new appointments were made to key roles on the University Executive from outside the University. In 2003, Lee Sanders joined as Registrar and Secretary from Warwick University. The next year, Professor Philip Jones, an academic lawyer and former Pro-Vice-Chancellor at Sheffield University, became Durham's first Deputy Vice-Chancellor. Both played a key role in shaping Durham's strategic vision to 2010, and in spearheading change.

The Council was also reshaped, with the active support of its committed lay members, into a slimmer, more efficient body at the start of 2006. There are also future plans for the reform of the Senate, which aim to ensure it retains a strong voice within a balanced system of governance.

The hardest decisions were perhaps those affecting some of Durham's academic departments. They included the smallest in the University, lacking critical mass, such as linguistics, politics, East Asian studies and the Institute of Middle Eastern and Islamic Studies (IMEIS). These were either absorbed within other parts of the University or, in the case of linguistics, transferred to Newcastle. For instance, politics and the IMEIS were merged within the Faculty of Social Sciences and Health, to create a stronger school concentrating on international relations. There was inevitably controversy. The dispersal of East Asian studies provoked particular uproar and a loyal group of alumni fought hard against the decision. Stockton too underwent a similar process of rationalisation. Courses failing to attract students were withdrawn. Concentrating on a narrower range of courses – medicine, biomedicine, primary education, applied psychology, business and finance – brought an increasing demand for places and higher quality applicants.

All this action was regarded as essential for the future of the University. It released £9 million for reinvestment within the University and also eliminated Durham's financial deficit. Crucially, a major part of these funds was invested in more academic posts or promoting current staff. In 2004, in its largest recruitment campaign for twenty years, the University made appointments to twenty-six posts, either for professors or lecturers, across thirteen departments. This ensured that Durham had the top calibre staff to complement the out-

Degree and honorary degree ceremonies: *left to right*, Kiri Te Kanawa and the former Archbishop of Canterbury, Robert Runcie,1982; Prince Charles,1998; graduation with Professor Tony Unsworth and graduands, 1998.

standing academics already working in the University. Such investment is crucial. The results can be seen in the breadth of research carried out in Durham. A typical list, from 1999, included the study of supply chain responsibilities, the effect of climate and habitat change on butterflies, building a new optical/infrared telescope for mapping the universe, the development of techniques and materials for nano-electronics, as well as projects covering innumerable aspects of theology, literature, history and the classics. Scientific excellence, through the accolade of Fellow of the Royal Society (FRS), is well represented on the staff, including Emeritus Professor Sir Arnold Wolfendale and Professors James Stirling, David Parker, Alan Martin, Carlos Frenk and Judith Howard, while Durham gained four new members of staff in the arts and humanities with the equivalent recognition of Fellow of the British Academy (FBA) in 2006, with the election of Emeritus Professor Rosemary Cramp and Professors James Dunn, Ray Hudson and Paul Sillitoe.

The impact was perhaps greatest in science, where, for instance, Durham had been the leading physics department in the country for several years. In 2005 international praise flooded in for the department's groundbreaking research into galaxy structure and formation in a joint project with researchers from Australia. Proving a direct link between the Big Bang theory and the galaxy, the hope is that this will lead to the discovery of how the cosmos was formed. The University's chemistry department is also widely acknowledged as among the top three in the country, and its work has earned praise from Nobel Prize winner Professor Bob Grubbs. The physics department too has an international research reputation. Among funded projects in the early twenty-first century is involvement in the UK's largest science project for thirty years, to create a soft X-ray diffractometer for observing the behaviour of electrons. Biomedical sciences has become one of the University's fastest growing departments. With an excellent rating for both research and teaching, it consolidated international recognition for its work in 2006 by winning a major funding award from the US National Institute of Health towards research into the control of malaria. The quality of all this research has made Durham the top science university in the UK, based on the frequency with which Durham research papers are cited in leading journals; and second in Europe only behind Zurich's Technical University. Durham is attracting increasing international attention. The University now has in excess of a hundred partnership agreements with other institutions, from the University of California in the USA to the University of Renmin in China. All this combined with the quality of the environment, attracts yet more high calibre scientists to the University and leads to further investment in first-class research facilities. Durham, in the words of the Dean of Science, is 'a scientific oasis'.[113] The University's prominence was recognised in the

Times Higher Education Supplement science citation table for 2005/06, where Durham was placed first in the UK and eighteenth in the world for the worldwide impact of its science research. This, with the breadth and depth of research carried out across the University, also saw Durham rated by the same journal as one of the top one hundred universities in the world.

Science is a good example of how outstanding research in one area produces spin-offs in related areas. The strength of basic science in Durham has led to cross-departmental links – and not just between chemistry, physics, biology and maths. Science within Durham has developed links with anthropology, geography and archaeology, as well as medicine and ethics. This fruitful crossing of boundaries has inspired Durham's Frontiers of Knowledge programme. This is based on the belief that there are three frontiers: one's own knowledge base, the frontiers between subjects where different knowledge bases interact, and the relationship between knowledge, public understanding and public policy. For instance, the development of energy policy has social, scientific, engineering, business and public policy implications, so it is important to develop a holistic, interlinked approach to such issues.

Bringing these strands together is one aim of the proposed Institute of Advanced Studies (IAS), which should be operational in 2007, where a wide mix of leading international experts in various fields will be able to interact while focusing on a single issue of joint interest. Professor Ash Amin, the executive director of IAS, stated that the Institute 'will identify, nurture and harness the world-class potential of Durham's researchers and link this into an international community of scholarship and practice'. Ten fellowships every semester will be awarded by the Institute to academics and public figures of renown, from both the UK and overseas.

Durham's involvement in developing interdisciplinary research is growing. For instance, as part of the University's 175th anniversary, the Institute for Hazard and Risk Research (IHRR) has been established within the department of geography, rated for its research as one of the four leading departments in the UK, and for its teaching as among the top ten. Focused on research into new forms of risk and hazard pervading every aspect of natural and social life, the Institute brings together researchers from the social, natural and engineering sciences. The Institute also demonstrates the importance to the University of generous benefactions: the building housing the Institute and the professorial chair are both funded by alumni of the University.

Excellence in science is matched by excellence in other departments throughout the University. Durham's outstanding archaeology department, rated as one of the top three in British universities, carries out research all over the world,

113 Personal interview with Dr Keith Orford, 17 November 2005.

Dancing in the Student Union.

Music Department.

from the UK to the Far East, and is frequently employed for advice by the development, environment and heritage sectors. The department of English studies is linked with a constantly expanding number of research centres, covering subjects such as art and humanities in health and medicine, seventeenth-century studies, and medieval and Renaissance studies. The latter is another example of interdisciplinary studies, involving leading historians, modern language scholars and philosophers. Theology and religion is perceived to be one of the leading departments of its type in the world, as well as one of the largest and most influential in the UK, ranging from biblical studies to the sociology and anthropology of religion. The history department too is well regarded, as is the department of law, listed as among the top eight in the country. Another notable research accolade came in 2005 when the Museums, Libraries and Archives Council conferred 'Designated' status on two of the collections at the University Library, in recognition of their international importance. This was one of only thirty-eight such awards made in England and Wales.

This all-round excellence in scholarship understandably attracts many more applicants than there are places. With ten applicants for every place, Durham's admission standards are high. The Vice-Chancellor and his team had never seen this as a bar to admitting students from a wider range of social backgrounds – Stockton had led the way in this commitment. The University was determined to tap some of the hidden potential among young people who had never considered studying for a degree. Durham began to market more widely what it had to offer, particularly on the University's doorstep in the north-east. For instance, summer schools were started for young students from secondary schools in the region. Many who attended would later apply to Durham and win places on their own merits. The University

sity also strengthened its school and college liaison team, and planned more school visits. Among several initiatives are the Student Targeted Aspiration Enhancement Scheme (STARS), for encouraging the entry into higher education of state school students in the north-east, and the Durham Educational Enhancement Programme, run in conjunction with the National Association for Gifted and Talented Youth, which organises events within the University for stimulating, stretching and encouraging able students. The colleges too are involved. Van Mildert founded the Young Persons' Project in 2001, which sends out college students to visit local schools, and organises a residential course for school students every Easter, giving them a first-hand insight into university life. In 2004 this targeted campaign succeeded in raising the proportion of entrants from state schools by 5 per cent to 67 per cent. Durham still had some way to go to achieve the benchmark set for it, which was 71 per cent in 2004, but this demonstrated a strong commitment to achieving it.

Another pressing need is investment in the refurbishment of existing facilities and the construction of new ones. While Stockton's teaching facilities are outstanding, the last new teaching block in Durham was completed in the 1970s. The University plans a rolling refurbishment programme to run through to 2016, combined with new development. The latter features new lecture theatres and a new earth sciences building on the science site, the relocation of the University administration from Old Shire Hall to the Mountjoy site, and new married accommodation for postgraduates on the location of the former Dryburn Hospital.

Sadly, in 2004, Durham's much-loved Chancellor, Sir Peter Ustinov, known for his sharp mind and easy manner, died. His death left a tremendous void and the University moved swiftly to find a successor. Bill Bryson, the US-born writer,